BE YOUR OWN CFO

THE ART OF CASH MANAGEMENT FOR SMEs

By John Bertrand

Published under licence 2012 by Searching Finance Ltd, 8 Whitehall Road, London W7 2JE, UK

ISBN: 978-1-907720-49-9

Typeset and designed by: Deirdré Gyenes

BE YOUR OWN CFO

THE ART OF CASH MANAGEMENT FOR SMEs

By John Bertrand

About the author

John Bertrand has over 30 years' expertise in banking, cash management, payments and technology, gained at Citibank, IBOS, ALLTEL and Misys in the USA and UK.

In this time John has created, developed, implemented and sold technology for front, middle and back offices in both banks and corporates. This includes redefining core banking for over 300 banks, developing cash management consulting, netting schemes, third party cash management, pooling and foreign exchange.

John has also worked with the financial authorities in the US (Federal Reserve), UK (Financial Services Authority) and Sweden (Finansinspektionen).

John is a Freeman of The City of London and has an MA from Warwick University in marketing and financing and a BSc (Hons) from City University in Civil Engineering.

About Searching Finance

Established in 2010, Searching Finance publishes books and reports on economics, politics and finance.

www.searchingfinance.com

CONTENTS

TABLES AND FIGURES

PREFACE

SMALL AND MEDIUM ENTERPRISES (SMEs) are vital to the economy. SMEs are often defined as companies with less than £50 million in annual turnover; there are 23 million SMEs in the European Union, representing 99% of all businesses and providing around 90 million jobs in the Single Market. However, finance is not easy to come by and SMEs need to seize any opportunities and incentives, as they are not offered willingly by banks.

Banks often categorise SMEs as a high credit risk, and because of their size SMEs are often the first to see a reduction or a calling in of their credit. SMEs' powers of negotiation with banks are fragmented and weak. SMEs have an essential role to play in delivering the economic growth required today, and governments therefore often have to take the lead, as the UK and USA are demonstrating.

In the UK, George Osborne, Chancellor of the Exchequer, noted in his Autumn Statement 2011:

> "With the strain on the financial system increasing, the important thing is to get credit flowing to Britain's small businesses.
>
> "Government can encourage many more of our small firms to export overseas for the first time. So we're doubling to 50,000 the number of SMEs we help and extending support to British mid-caps which can

> some-times lack the overseas ambition of their German equivalents.
>
> "Government has developed with the Bank of England a mechanism to allocate funding to different banks based on how much they increase both net and gross lending to firms. And there will be a clear audit trail to ensure the banks comply – for we will use the experience of the European Investment Bank's Loans for SMEs program here in the UK to ensure it works.
>
> "From April 2012, anyone investing up to £100,000 in a qualifying new start-up business will be eligible for income tax relief of 50% – regardless of the rate at which they pay tax."

In the US, President Obama noted on April 13, 2012: "Small businesses are the backbone of our economy and the cornerstones of our nation's promise. The same is true throughout the western hemisphere, where the small business sector plays a critical role in job creation and broad-based economic growth."

The President also reiterated his commitment to expanding available financing resources for SMEs by catalysing greater private sector lending to SMEs to address the estimated $160-190 billion credit gap these businesses face in Latin America and the Caribbean.

SMEs are essential to stimulate growth and prosperity. Finance is the SMEs' route to becoming the new elite in the business world. The goal is to use all financial options that are available and make sense to you to your best advantage. This book will show you what to do to ensure you continue to have cash to have the confidence to become great.

INTRODUCTION

Cash management is a broad term which covers the usage of cash across a wide range of activities which includes, at the basic level, paying or getting paid by someone. It is the use of cash on hand or of cash due that can bring prosperity, or if not looked after, that can cause misery. As Charles Dickens wrote over 100 years ago:

> "Annual income twenty pounds, annual expenditure nineteen six, result happiness. Annual income twenty pounds, annual expenditure twenty pound ought and six, result misery."

Today, in the current environment even the least financially interested or literate company owner or Board member needs to know how much cash is available and what is expected to arrive and leave in the next three months. The majority of SMEs go into receivership and bankruptcy through lack of liquidity.

The issue when liquidity dries up is the need to access cash quickly; however, as the old banker's adage goes, "If you want a quick decision, it's no". Consequently, cash has to be treated with the understanding that you and only you can manage it to your requirements. Being without cash causes the market to extract the maximum price for providing the cash to relieve this often temporary inconvenience. Unfortunately, the cash management skills of most SMEs come from 'on the job' training and learning from experience. Often an SME has had limited exposure to the cash management function. Many of the textbooks are quite technical, focusing in on particular subjects written by specific subject experts. Furthermore, it's quite common for people not to be confident with their numeracy, having undergone a school education that has left them believing that showing 'x' to be a number is an oxymoron.

The aim of this book

The aim of this book is to provide guidance on new ways to ensure cash is ready to deal with whatever happens in the market. It will help guide SMEs through the myriad of complications and complexities of cash management offered by the banks and others in the current financial storm. It aims to make liquidity understandable, and offers guidelines on how to enhance the current situation. By having a greater insight into the banking, payment and trade infrastructures, better decisions can be made. These decisions will lead to increased satisfaction and confidence, while driving the efficiency and effectiveness of cash in the business.

Technology drives change

Technology such as smartphones and PCs now makes information readily available from the banks to the SMEs. Brett King of MovenBank noted in March 2012 that in the number of UK bank branches has contracted 42% over the last 20 years, yet balances were being accessed 20x more frequently in a given month.

The average British person visits the branch bank two to three times per month and 15 to 20% do not visit the branch at all. The use of technology has also changed how frequently balance information is checked:

Account balance by:

Paper statement	1x per month
Internet	7x
Mobile	20x

The issue for the SMEs is that all banks have different reporting formats. Consequently, if you have more than one bank account at different banks, then the consolidation of information at the same time is difficult. Banks have viewed the use of proprietary formats as a market differentiator. It is difficult to switch from one bank to another as the banks' legacy systems prevent easy movement of the activities connected to the bank account, e.g. direct debits.

Real-time banking and payments

The world is moving to real time. For example, gambling has now moved into 'in play' betting; that means that odds are given on the next event which could occur imminently in a particular sporting event. In the UK, 'Faster Payments' provides instant transfer for up to £100,000 from a mobile telephone. The payment is secure, easy to use and irrevocable – no more bounced cheques. In the Netherlands, according to iDeal, online payments have increased:

Year	2009	2010	2011	Year 2011 change
Volume in millions	45	69	94	+36%

The Netherland's iDeal is the mechanism for using a bank account to pay for products and services securely online through e-banking. iDeal allows the money to be taken from the bank account. This method of taking money directly from the bank account is taking 58% of the transactions in the Netherlands. iDeal bank account transfers is followed in popularity by debit cards (17%) and credit cards (12%). The use of mobile is also accelerating in the Netherlands:

Year	2009	2010	2011
Mobile usage	30%	35%	50%
Internet banking			94%

iDeal noted that smartphones are intrinsically more secure than PCs and the main security risk comes from the user of the smartphone himself.

The trend for online activity is extremely strong, with the biggest indicator being the Facebook community growing from 34 million accounts (people) in 2008 to 825 million by 2013. These people will need to transact. Today, they may be doing so offline, but the onward march of PayPal (which functions as a warehouse account – see Chapter 3) with its growth of $100 billion in payments in 2011, of which $4 billion came from a mobile phone payments, suggests this too is inevitable. PayPal estimates that in 2012 mobile payments will double to $8 billion.

Other driving forces

All that is needed is for all the participants to be engaged. The banks, payment providers, payment schemes and channels are moving over to providing automatic and timely knowledge of where the money is at any point in time - not only domestically, but also internationally, and not just one bank, but all banks. The fiscal crisis has focused the attention of the creditworthiness of banks. Many SMEs have a better credit rating than their bank. In Sweden in the 1990s the banking collapse saw a change in behaviour. People and companies went from just having one bank to having many. The treasury department of the Swedish construction firm Skanska ($100 billion in revenue) believes that, to protect itself, the company should set a limit of no more than 33% of its cash with any one bank. That means having three different banks looking after deposits once those deposits become significant in size for the SME.

SMEs have experienced how banks have reacted to the fiscal crisis over the last few years through the calling in and repricing upwards of credit. Many banks have clauses which state something like: "The overdraft is repayable on demand. This means that we may at any time require you to immediately repay the whole overdraft". This behaviour, like the Swedes experienced in the 1990s, suggests a strategy of using more than one bank for your cash management would be prudent

A further series of events have pushed cash management into the forefront of attention in the world today:

1. Liquidity concerns and cash cushions (the regulators want a robust fiscal system that can withstand a bank failing without a government bailout);
2. No growth economies (especially in Europe, at +2% versus +6% in developing countries – source: *The Independent*, 2012);
3. Tight credit markets (a AAA credit score is becoming rare through the downgrading of banks and governments);
4. Recapitalisation of banks to meet new global standards (Wells Fargo estimates that Basel III will increase their capital needs by 25% by the time it is fully operational in 2019);
5. New legal regulations and compliance, especially regarding withholding tax on people holding money offshore – starting with the US's Foreign Account Tax Compliance Act (FATCA) – see Chapter 2).

These events cause banks to react and this reaction, often centrally initiated, causes the availability of credit and the interest levels available to SMEs to be negatively affected. In the UK, the British Bankers Association reported a decline of 11% in overdrafts and personal loans year-on-year from December 2010 to 2011.

The due diligence involved in granting of credit also becomes more intense and time-consuming. Recent activities, especially compute- generated, take priority over years of previous documented behaviour and relationships. Liquidity gives a level of independence and financial security to the SME and that needs to be maintained.

Managing cash flow

Regardless of the size of the cash flow, it needs to be managed. Not managing it or managing it badly creates negativity and stress. Managing it well brings extra rewards and increases well-being and positivity. It also can be the divide between success and failure, with all aspects being equal.

In addition, banks have changed their approach towards how money is managed. Gone are the days of tolerance and flexibility. They are approaching cash management with a zero tolerance attitude that would make a police state smile. No arrests, only big fines for the smallest transgressions. For example, moving more money out of your account than is present could easily result in a hefty fine, sometimes 10x the amount moved. So watch out, as it is not going to get easier.

The key for SMEs in this era is to make certain accounts do not go negative. Most banks charge fees for credit provision, often up to 20% per annum, which are completely disproportionate to the interest they pay, often less than 0.5% per annum. Banks have also taken a zero tolerance approach to credit, with many reducing the credit line available and/or increasing the interest rate being levied. Credit from banks is becoming scarce and opening the door to non-banks to provide credit. These include asset based financing, pledged collateral and short-term loans. The cost of these types of financing can often exceed 20%, with the shorter loans exceeding 100%.

Liquidity is key as the world struggles back from the financial abyss. Households worldwide are reducing their indebtedness. The US has repaid 11% in consumer debt since the start of the crisis. The Federal Reserve in March 2012 reported corporate cash balances continued to grow to $2.23 trillion, an $845 billion increase since Q1 2009. The UK, the Nordic countries and Spain have seen debt as a percentage of household income also in decline. An investment pyramid and credit ladder review helps gauge the assets, the liquidity and credit exposure of the SME (see Chapter 7).

As a result of the new Basel III proposals, banks need to recapitalise. Cash cushions against future falls are being prepared. Cash cushions are being mandated by the authorities to help prevent banks from failing if and when fiscal events prove challenging. Such considerations should be applied to the SME to help create a renewed confidence in facing the financial future. Managing cash is now not a sideline, but a main part of the business for the SMEs and, thanks to the smartphone, an integral part of life for most people.

The Aberdeen Group reported in January 2012 that 82% of companies have increased their focus on cash management. The PwC Global Treasury Survey 2010 noted the proportion of participants rating cash management as highly important has doubled from 35% to 70%.

The top 20% performers in Aberdeen's cash management study have the following characteristics:

- 28% align the Treasurer with the management team, often reporting to the Board;
- 53% are less likely to rely on manual procedures and spreadsheets;
- 69% are more likely than their peers to have Straight Through Processing (STP);
- 88% are likely to have automated reconciliation of the bank accounts.

One of the most neglected aspects of cash management is accurate cash forecasting. According to a Schmidt CS Survey, 79% of companies polled still used spreadsheets for cash forecasting. HSBC's own survey of its corporate customers found that 42% rely on manual forecasts, something with which 80% are dissatisfied.

The focus on cash is on the rise since the financial crisis and has propelled company cash balances to new record heights. Cash and equivalents in the top 1,000 European companies for 2010 increased 18% over 2009, as noted by REL Consulting. The cash holdings ot the Top US 1,000 Companies increased by 6% in 2010 over 2009. The 2010 US cash figure of $850 billion was 75% higher than 2007, the beginning of the financial crisis. In addition, since 2008, cash in the supply chain has increased by €183.5 billion as debtors have slowed payments by an average of 4.3 days of sale. Companies are creating their own cash cushions.

The rising cost of banking and credit

Besides, as the British Bankers' Association has stated, it is down to customers to make sure they are not caught out by extra charges – that same body that saw and supported its banking members who charged Payment Protection Insurance (PPI) to most people looking for credit. Finally, after a long, drawn-out legal appeal the banks admitted they were wrong and have allocated £10 billion to compensate their clients. However, it is up to the customer and not the banks to identify who has been mis-sold to, the amount in question, produce the evidence and then claim back the money.

Similarly, around the world banks are looking to charge for any services or extras they can in a drive for more revenue. Banks are offering minimum interest rates on money held in instant access bank accounts. When granting credit, which is becoming scarce as many banks are over-extended and also have to recapitalise due to new regulations, the rates of interest are increasing.

The rise in and variety of fees surrounding the bank account is growing. Bank accounts are now being offered with a package of benefits such as travel insurance. Transaction charges by the type of payments being made are wide, with international costs being far more expensive than domestic payments. Extras such as requests for duplicate statements and alert texts are being priced. Some of these practices, such as the proposed fees on debit cards put forward by Bank of America, have seen a public outcry. The alternatives to a bank account – a 'warehouse' or third party account, are starting to look attractive from a cost point of view.

In addition to reducing credit exposure, banks are also looking to SMEs to help rebuild their finances. Now more than ever SMEs need to be aware of their money and to act to ensure that this money works for them. For example, any requests, errors or unknowing movements of money resulting in authorised overdrafts will incur fees from the banks. Over only a few weeks, these fees can exceed the interest paid on savings for a whole year.

Banks create their own cash cushions

Under the Basel III proposals, banks need to create a cash cushion of 2.5% included in the capital structure. The difference between Basel I and Basel III looks like an additional 25% in new capital for most banks.

This does not bode well for credit availability from banks. Banks with a 10% capital ratio can lend 10 times their capital base. As an illustration, having raised $1 billion in new capital, the bank could lend $10 billion. The new capital increase is to shore up the existing position; therefore the only new lending capabilities come from the maturing of debt. A new capital ratio of 15% reduces the amount of credit a bank can offer from $10 billion to $6.7 billion, a loss of lending of $3.3 billion to the community.

Cash and liquid instruments are kings. The challenge is where to keep the cash and make money off that money. This is becoming harder, as in January 2011 Germany sold six-month bills at a negative interest rate yield. The investment pyramid ranks risk against return, with the safest and most liquid at the base. The higher up the pyramid, the higher the risk and the lower the liquidity (see Chapter 8). At the top of the pyramid liquidity is virtually nil. Any forced move to take liquidity out of those assets held at the top will result in the assets being sold at a heavy discount to the market, hence the phrase 'fire sale'. For longer-term cash cushions, Cash Managers should consider strong currencies and gold with the appropriate stop-losses.

Both are highly liquid and have shown past appreciation rates in double digits.

The move towards non-banks

The key for cash management now is to make absolutely certain that accounts do not go negative. Most banks charge fees for credit provision, often up to 20% per annum, that are completely disproportionate to the interest they pay, which is often less than 0.5% per annum. Banks have also taken a zero tolerance approach to credit, with many reducing the credit line available and/or increasing the interest rate being levied. Credit from banks is becoming scarce, and this is opening doors to non-banks to provide credit. These include asset-based financing, pledged collateral and short-term loans with funding coming from the non-bank sector. Often this sector is funded by banks which are taking the risk on one company. This company lends out to many companies at a higher interest rate. The cost of these types of financing can often exceed 20%, with the shorter loans exceeding 100%.

This move away from the banking community to non-banks is beginning to accelerate across the bank product range. For example:

- Credit is being offered by new companies offering secured and unsecured loans especially through asset finance – rates higher than the banks;
- Savings: Sweden permits new companies to offer certificates or bonds backed by callable assets and these are paying 6% against the banks;
- Payments: Warehouse account companies such as PayPal allow payments to be made at any time with credit to a bank account in a maximum of three days. In the UK Barclays has just enabled payments to be made from a smartphone on a virtually instantaneous basis. Both PayPal and Barclays use existing banking infrastructures to make payments easy and convenient.

The importance of automation

Technology and ready access to data is driving the product sets away from banks and managing cash requires anyone to find the best and safest product. Banks can no longer believe that while they have the bank account they have the business.

There is a push is to remove the paperwork out of the banking process. The reason is that paper has to be processed by hand. The manual cost is far more than it is to move the data electronically. Also manual processes are time-consuming and can be error-prone. Banks worldwide are going digital. This is also true for large businesses, which increasingly are insisting on e-invoicing.

In addition, payments should become more electronic and instant. This is already happening as the cheque usage is falling across the world. Cheque processing also attracts a disproportionate amount of fraud. The use of direct debits is a great way to collect recurring money owned on the due date.

The European Union, through law, has forced the banks into providing euro payments on D+1 from January 2012. D+1 is payment within a maximum of 48 hours or from now until tomorrow. The EU is also keen to have a common direct debit across Europe (SEPA Direct Debit – see Chapter 9) and has at last announced an end date of February 2014. Now the banks must comply.

CHAPTER 1
THE THREE LEVELS OF CASH MANAGEMENT

Questions for SME directors

- What is our cash position now?
- How many bank accounts do we have?
- Who do we know at the bank?
- Are any of the accounts running near to or below zero?

Key considerations

- Cash management starts simply but can quickly become complex;
- A couple of weeks' of overdraft charges can wipe out a year's worth of interest;
- Free bank accounts are in decline and account fees are growing;
- Technology is becoming a significant part of the process;
- A minimum of two bank accounts is recommended for SMEs.

Introduction

THE THREE LEVELS of cash management are:

1: Domestic cash management;
2: International cash management; and
3: Global cash management.

Cash management starts simply enough and then grows in complexity as the company grows and changes. The first bank account is usually registered in a single currency; this may be followed by development steps to meet the increasing globalisation of people and businesses. The first step is local cash management, often referred to as 'domestic cash management'. Once another currency becomes active, the step becomes 'international cash management', followed by the final step of 'global cash management'.

Within each level, there are several stages of functionality and complexity that have developed to meet the organisation's requirements and growth stage, from a simple transactional bank account for accounts payable and receivable, through to sophisticated and bespoke cash management services for global businesses.

- Stage 1: Simple bank account;
- Stage 2: Bank account with technology;
- Stage 3: Bank account with investment rules;
- Stage 4: Bank account with overdraft facilities;
- Stage 5: Multiple banks with more than one bank account in the same currency;
- Stage 6: International cash management services with more than one currency account;
- Stage 7: Global cash management.

Domestic cash management

Cash management starts very simply with a bank account.

A SME opens the account with a bank to begin business. For a company the initial reason is to pay suppliers (creditors) and receive funds from sales (debtors). These two activities are termed the accounts payable and the accounts receivable and are the financial heart of the company.

Figure 1.1: Simple domestic cash management

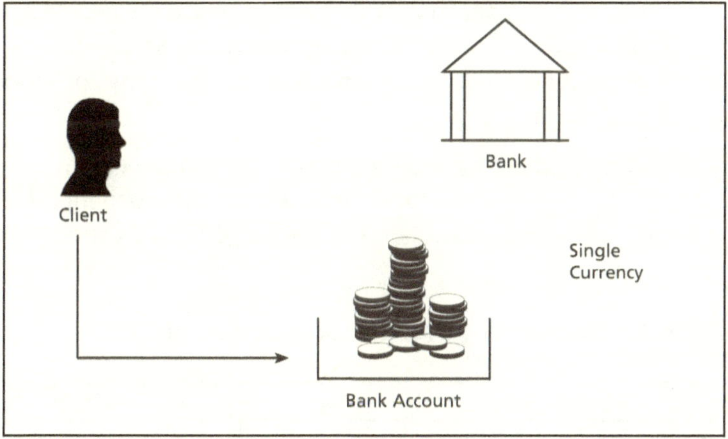

Source: IBS Publishing

An individual opens a bank account to have the ability to make and receive payments, save money and have the ability to borrow money. In addition the majority of employees pay into a bank account, with fewer and fewer paying staff in cash. It is estimated that by 2018, UK companies paying cash will be less than 2% of the total. In the UK in 2010 it was estimated 1,000,000 adults did not have a bank account. In the USA, the Federal Deposit Insurance Corporation reported in 2009 the unbanked represented 17.9% of the population and 7.7% of households.

Bank charges on the rise

In the US and elsewhere, banks historically have given their customers free banking. But now bank charges are being made for accounts, and this trend looks like it will continue and spread. Examples in the US include:

- Wells Fargo – $5 per month for using cheques and $6.95 for online bill payment;
- Citicorp – $8 per month if five transactions or more are made;
- Chase – $12 per month if the customer does not maintain $1,500 in the bank account, or $5,000 across deposit accounts or does not make a minimum of $500 in deposits.

Similarly in the UK, fees for bank accounts are being introduced. The terms and conditions along with benefits are reflected in the monthly charges that range from £5 to £19.50 per month.

Table 1.1: Features of UK bank accounts 2009, 2010

	2009	2010	Change
Average interest rate paid on £1,000	0.87%	0.61%	+30.00%
Number of banks NOT paying interest	23.00%	59.00%	+157.00%
Average authorised overdraft rate per annum	14.10%	14.90%	+6.00%
Number of paid packaged accounts	54.00%	69.00%	+28.00%
Average monthly fee for packaged accounts	£13.62	£15.37	+13.00%

Source: Defaqto

One in five adults in the UK now has a packaged account – the regular bank account surrounded by a group of services such as travel insurance, shop discounts, etc. that the bank offers for monthly fee. Since 2010, the UK banks have paid 30% less interest on the accounts still carrying interest; 60% of accounts do not pay interest, up from 23%, packaged services has grown by 28% and the price of these packages has grown by 13%. The average authorised rate for overdrafts looks set to rise by 35% as the major UK clearers are raising the interest level to just under 20% throughout 2011. The response to these trends by the UK population is remarkably low; just 3.8% changed bank accounts in 2011, according to the Independent Commission on Banking.

The ICB and the Payment Council in the UK have agreed to bring in a guarantee scheme by September 2013 that bank accounts can be moved in seven business days against the current barriers to account switching which are taking a minimum of seven days. The guarantee includes:

- The old account remains open, and the customer uses it in exactly the same way, until the end of the seventh day. On the eighth working day, their new account will be fully operational, and any remaining credit in their old account transferred across;
- The customer will receive whatever they need to operate the new account, like a debit card, PIN and cheque book within those seven working days;
- The customer's new bank will arrange for all their incoming and outgoing payment instructions to be redirected from the old account to the new one;
- The customer's balance will be transferred to the new Account;
- Any payments sent to the old account on or after the seventh working day will be automatically 'caught' and moved on to the new account;
- The customer will not suffer if there are any bank errors;

- The old current account will be closed at the end of the process.

In addition the ICB is aiming at increasing competition for the four existing banks which dominate the local UK banking market.

Suggested fees for the use of debit cards (these often come automatically with the bank account) suggested by US banks have come under heavy criticism. In the UK, debit cards were encouraged to help displace cheques, and as such, largely remain free to use. However, the UK Government has highlighted the passing on of fees charged by the card companies to online retailers which in turn pass an increased fee for their usage to the customer. The goal is to outlaw such increasing of fees for using debit and credit cards to buy goods and services and automatically adding them to the bill.

Bank accounts are not free any more and companies tend to pay more than consumers for them. Most companies are offered bank accounts based on a package of services with a transaction prices list tied to volume and type.

It is also clear, given the disparity in interest rates for savings – 0.61% per year against 20% on an authorised overdraft limit (unauthorised overdrafts are even more expensive) that a couple of weeks' of overdraft charges can wipe out a year's worth of interest.

Consequently today's cash management ethos is to make certain the probability of a bank account going into an overdraft position is virtually zero.

The bank account is the payment gateway to the banking communities' payment infrastructure and the start of any cash management is the opening of a bank account. The bank account is the gateway to the local bank's payment and clearing systems and a bank's correspondent banking network for international payments. Banks, under their banking licence, are permitted to pay and credit accounts from their pool of money. The pool is a combination of everyone's money in the bank. Each bank can lend up to a certain amount before being restricted by capital requirements. Capital requirements for banks have been increasing over the years. Under Basel II, the banking regulators were looking for 8% (2006); now under Basel III (2012 onwards), the requirement is 10.5%. This is the amount of capital banks have to keep on hand to cover unexpected financial conditions.

Figure 1.2: Account opening process

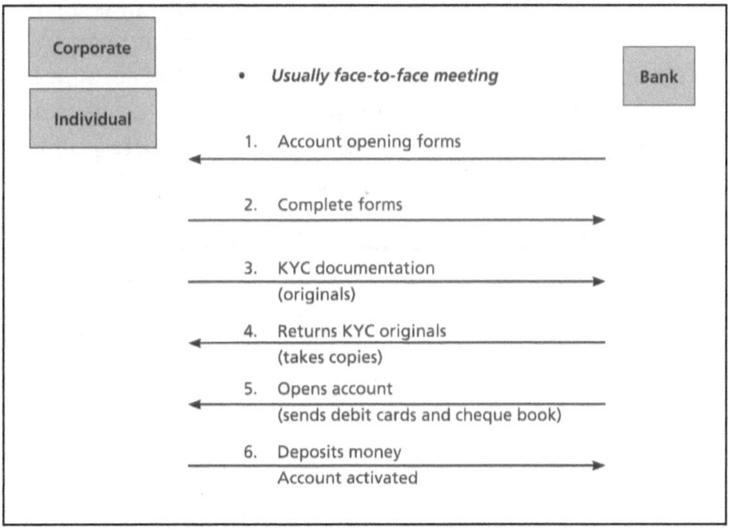

Source: Author

Domestic cash management stages

Domestic cash management covers stages 1–5 and provides increasing levels of complexity of features.

Stage 1: Simple bank account

Key features:

- Account in a single currency;
- Access through the branch;
- Ability to collect money;

- Ability to pay money if cash is in the account;
- Payments made by cheque, electronic transfer or Automated Clearing House (ACH);
- Branch foreign exchange rates offered for any infrequent currency movements.

The bank account is in a single currency and opened at a branch or bank business office. Banks handling business banking often have separate areas for their business clients. The need to deposit payment by cheque leads the corporate to use the local branch of the bank where its bank account has been opened. The account allows the business client to use the domestic clearing system and the bank's correspondent network for international payments.

Figure 1.3: Simple bank account – domestic

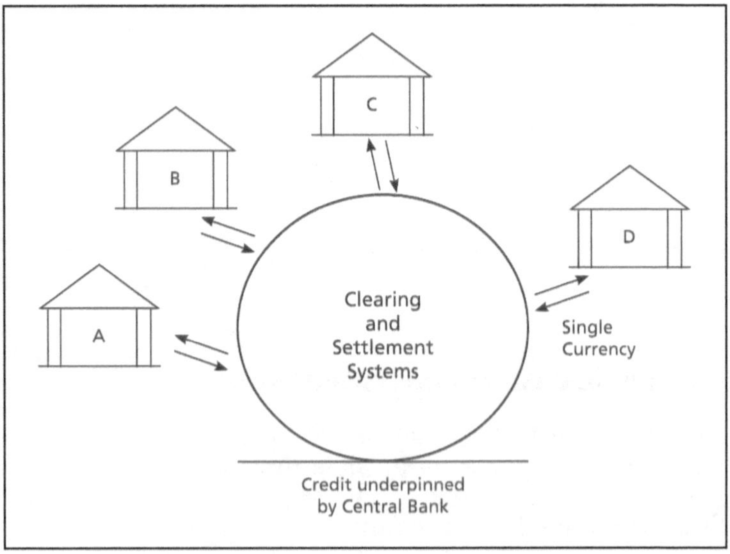

Source: IBS Publishing

Figure 1.4: Simple bank account – international

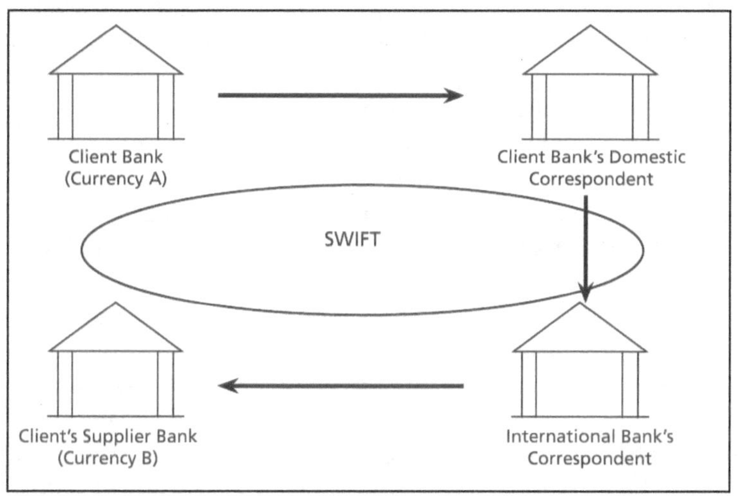

Source: IBS Publishing

Stage 2: Bank account with technology

Key features:

- As Stage 1 with:
    - E-banking software – either internet or proprietary channels;
    - Mobile banking using smart phone (m-payments).

E-banking now the preferred approach

The US was probably the first to start electronic banking (e-banking) closely followed by Europe. Europe was the first with Automatic Teller Machines (ATMs). ATMs and e-banking were the first products to enable the bank account to become 'self-service'; people other than bank staff could access i.e. the account.

The use of e-banking started in the 1980s with priority systems from each of the major corporate banks. These systems were expensive to build and maintain, but they met the business market need to look after their money. It is still startling that most companies fail not though poor products, management or business strategy, but through cash flow. Consequently the need for cash management has been a growing concern for both domestic and international businesses.

The internet has replaced the need for priority communication networks, which the major banks used as their competitive edge in the 1980s and 1990s in offering cash management business. The sheer scale of telecommunication growth and usage has enabled any bank to enter the e-banking market.

Historically the larger banks held the skills to create their own e-banking and cash management software. Now many software companies are using XML, and open software computer languages and can provide these services on a license or as an Application Service Provider (ASP) using internal or cloud technology. Cloud technology is starting to absorb ASPs, making the application and infrastructure a single purchase. In addition smartphone applications – iPhone, Blackberry and Android – are starting to appear; for example, one app can view bank balances held at a number of banks.

Banks are starting to make e-banking the preferred approach as the information comes and goes in a fully automated format. This makes it easier to receive and deliver information to the client.

Mobile banking and smartphones

Smartphones are becoming the device of choice for many customers. Today the smartphone has more functionality than most desktop computers. In the UK, 50% of the UK population has a smartphone. Smartphones now dominate the market, with Android (50%) and Apple (25%) as its leaders. (Source: Kantor) The remainder of the market is taken by Windows phones (Microsoft and Nokia) and Blackberry (the first phone to push email to the user).

In the UK, by 2013 it is estimated that up to 20% of a bank's activity will come via the mobile phone. The trend among a number of banks is to add m-banking to their e-banking offering so the client has one interface, regardless of device.

In February 2012 Barclays UK launched Pingit, an app that allows an owner of a Barclays bank account who also has a smartphone to send up to £300 ($450) per day to another bank account. Non-Barclays customers with a current account can only receive payments at this time. In its first two days, the app was downloaded 20,000 times. The British Bankers Association (BBA) noted that there were 43.6 million internet bank registrations in the UK in 2011 (up from 32.1 million in 2007).

The UK Payments Council has commissioned VocaLink, the manager of the UK automated clearing house (ACH), to build a central database that will allow bank customers to link their mobile phone number to their account for person-to-person mobile payments. This will offer a standard service to current bank account holders, allowing intra-operability across the banking sector. Unlike e-banking where each bank has a proprietary standard, mobile payments in the UK will have a common and secure database.

Stage 3: Bank account with investment rules

Key features:

- As Stage 1 with:
    - Interest paid on certain balances, often in a separate savings account;
    - Higher interest paid on higher yielding 'market' instruments;
    - Time-extended investments based on account balances for greater yield.

Stage 4: Bank account with overdraft facilities

Key features:

- As Stage 1 or 2 with:

- Overdraft facility allowing the account to be overdrawn to a set level;
- Loan facilities after 'credit review'.

In a 2009 study by the University of Warwick, the use of bank overdrafts was down 20% from 2005-08 as compared to 2001-04. In 2007-08, 88% of SMEs felt discouraged from applying for an overdraft as compared to 12% in 2005-07. Margins also doubled, with average risk rated firms paying 4.2% above the base rate in 2008; this trend has continued, with bank margins on many overdrafts for SMEs going into double digits.

A similar study in 2004 showed the use of banking products in the US and UK were largely similar.

Table 1.2: Comparison of financial products in the UK and US

	US SSBF[1] (1998)	UK SMEF[2] (2004)
Any loan[3]	55%	65%
Personal credit card	45%	28%
Business credit card	33%	34%
Current account	94%	97%
Deposit account	22%	41%

Notes:
1. US Survey of Small Business Finance
2. Small and Medium Enterprises Finances
3. For the US, any loan denotes using any of the following: credit lines; mortgages; vehicle loans; equipment loans; or capital leases. For the UK any loan denotes using any one of: overdrafts; term loans; asset finance; or asset-based finance.

Stage 5: Multiple banks with more than one bank account in the same currency

Key features:

- As Stage 1, 2, or 3 with:
  - More than one account in the local currency;
  - Account consolidator, especially sweeping, topping and zero balances.

Multibanking occurs as the corporation grows. A growing company attracts different banks. As the late Steve Jobs, CEO of Apple, noted: "When JPMorgan sent people to meet me, I knew Apple had joined the big boys". Neither the bank nor the company wants to be reliant solely on each other. Consequently, multinational and very large national companies have more than one bank. However, the majority of SMEs in the UK have a single banking relationship.

It is prudent to have more than one bank account as different banks at different times expand or decrease levels and fees on services based on their own requirements

Banks offer, regardless of country, some form of the above under the general term of domestic cash management. The switch to electronic access (e-banking) is based on the e-readiness of the country (see Table 1:3, Top 20 country e-readiness scale) and those banks that have invested in electronic cash management. Where the electronic infrastructure does not exist or is not used, then companies use physical receipt and delivery usually around the bank's branch or business offices.

Table 1.3: EIU 2010 digital economy rankings and scores

1.	Sweden	8.49/10	11.	Canada	8.05
2.	Denmark	8.41	12.	Taiwan	7.99
3.	United States	8.41	13.	South Korea	7.94
4.	Finland	8.36	14.	United Kingdom	7.89
5.	Netherlands	8.36	15.	Austria	7.88
6.	Norway	8.24	16.	Japan	7.85
7.	Hong Kong	8.22	17.	Ireland	7.82
8.	Singapore	8.22	18.	Germany	7.80
9.	Australia	8.21	19.	Switzerland	7.72
10.	New Zealand	8.07	20.	France	7.67

Source: Economist Intelligence Unit

The banks that have invested in e-banking have done so in such a way that the interface between the bank and the customer is unique to that bank. Consequently, using more than one bank means that consolidation at the company needs two or more interfaces. Few countries have insisted on a multibank format/interface standard, with the exception of Germany. German banks operate in a multibank environment so only one interface is needed for their banking community. The need to build interfaces restricts the flow of information within a country tending the community to focus the banking activity on to one bank for ease of use.

Complexity increases as company grows

As the company grows, the need for additional bank accounts becomes a necessity. The accounts are opened for a variety of reasons, but the need to make the most out of the money is still there. It is here that the complexity of cash management begins to increase and banks begin to specialise. The first step is to bring the accounts of the company together. In the simplest form it is the mailing-out of the bank accounts to the same address, or showing the accounts on e-banking as separate accounts. The bank does not try to work with the accounts as if they belonged to one company.

Technology and processes

It is here the technology and processes being applied by certain banks within a particular country that start to earn them a name for cash management. In addition, the availability of inexpensive software to assist companies in reconciling their bank accounts has made companies keener to have the banks develop more sophisticated techniques. This has lead to competition from banks outside the domestic country for the larger companies' banking business. The key technique is the automated movement of funds between all the accounts so that no one account generates overdraft charges should one of the accounts become overdrawn when another has more than enough to cover the shortage. It is similar on the investment side when consolidating the money enables the company to generate a greater level of interest payment

Figure 1.5: More than one company bank account (single currency) – simple

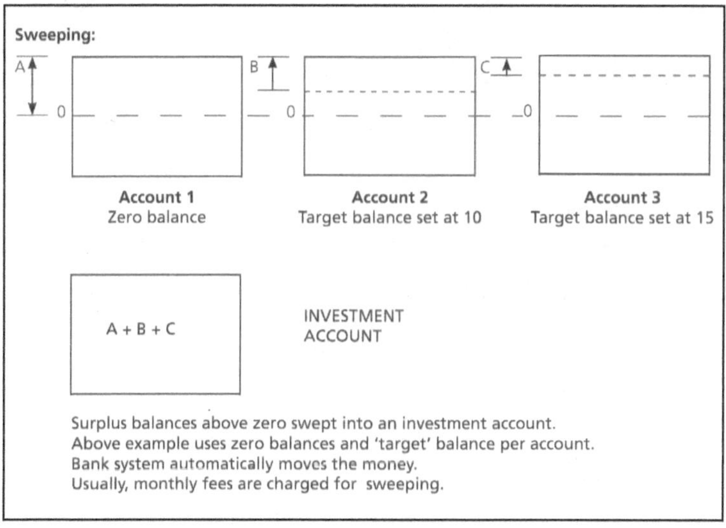

Source: IBS Publishing

Figure 1.6: More than one company bank account (single currency) – alternative

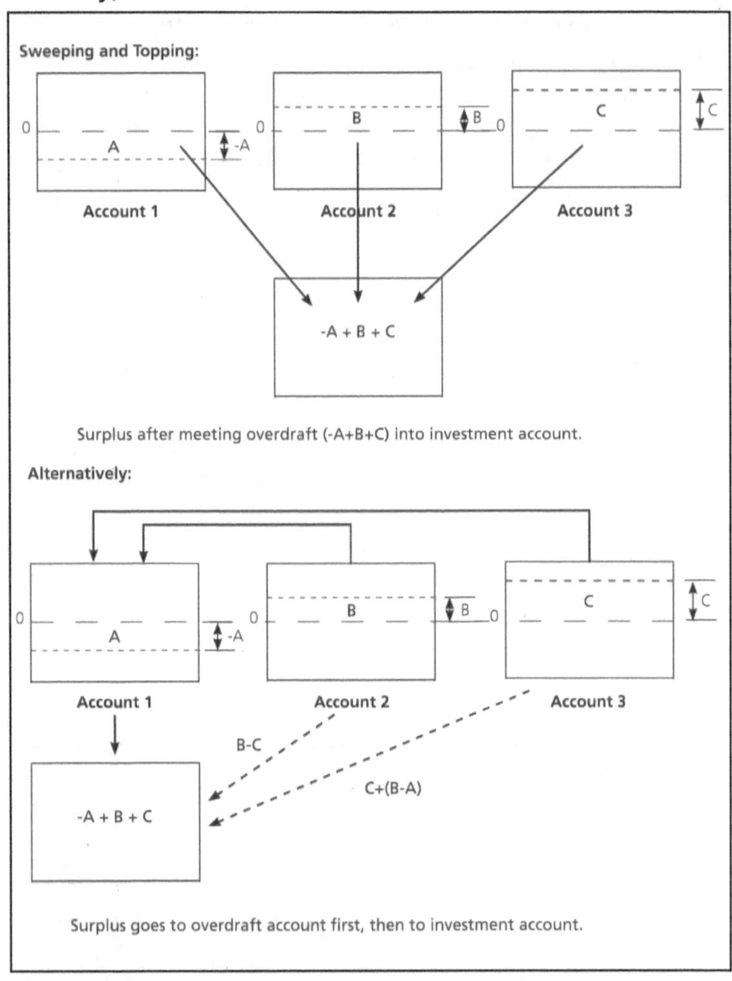

Source: IBS Publishing

The account consolidation also manages the billing. The levels of transactions by accounts are totalled and matched against an agreed to level of transaction charges. It is these companies with strong transactional business that are valuable to banks. These businesses, providing the credit situation between them and the bank is not locked, can offer their banking business for competitive bids.

Competitive bidding for banking business

The competitive bidding process starts with a RFP (Request for Proposal), which is prepared by the company or its consultants. The RFP covers the transactional volumes and the details of when, where and how they occur. Details are also provided on the types of payment channels being used. The RFP will include SLAs (service level agreements) and the business will expect the bank to sign up to them with penalties should they fall below the set standards. RFPs tend to come from the major users of cash management services and may request the bank to outsource the process for the business with the appropriate controls in place.

International cash management

Stage 6:International cash management services with more than one currency account

Key features:

- As Stage 5 with:
    - Accounts in more than one currency in more than one country;
    - Credit lines in more than one country;
    - FX credit limits;
    - Access to corporate desk or electronic FX real-time updates;
    - Derivatives;
    - Netting;
    - Pooling.

As soon as a company opens a bank account with a different currency it has moved into the world of international cash management. For the first time, the business has to consider ongoing foreign exchange, exposure management, netting, pooling, tax and regulatory environments. The level of cash management complexity has exploded and continues to accelerate the more international business the company adds.

The addition of a second currency not only layers in a new set of services, but is also more profitable for the bank. Banks have historically earned considerable more on 'international' transactions. International payments, for example, are often 10 times more expensive than domestic ones, and these payments have to pass through another country's payment infrastructure. This infrastructure often requires additional information and a change in message format. International payments can take far longer, increasing the float to the banking system.

The European Union has put in place an initiative (Single Euro Payments Area – SEPA) to standardise payments across the eurozone. SEPA mandates to the banks a set of standard procedures to enable the euro to act like a domestic currency across country borders.

As each country has its own existing and working payment settlement systems operating under each countries own regulation, the change needed to meet a global standard is massive and is slowly coming.

One aspect of the SEPA is the adoption of standards on a global basis, which can be seen by the increasing use of the IBAN (international bank account number) and BIC (bank identifier code – although the EU has just ruled that the BIC code is no longer required by law. The law is based around the IBAN.). Each bank has established its own BIC, which is SWIFT-compliant. With the IBAN each company's bank account can be readily pointed to and payments directed from any account, anywhere.

This does remove tremendous inefficiency out of the international banking system, which is good for commerce and a mixed blessing for the banks. The banks want to remove the inefficiencies – repairing international payments, which is a small industry in itself, which the banks incur the expense – but removing the inefficiencies of the payment processes costs the banks money in reduced float.

To gain these efficiencies, businesses now need to add BIC and IBAN numbers on their invoices to their clients. That is, more information is needed on the invoicing to international based clients and suppliers. As BIC and IBAN are long streams of numbers the chances of them being accurately transcribed manually are low. Hence businesses and banks are changing to provide information electronically.

On the international side, SWIFT (a banking community owned infrastructure) provides data from other banks using a dedicated message type. Companies can receive their balances and transactions from multiple banks provided their bank offers it and, in turn, the companies' international banks have installed SWIFT functionality.

Banks like business, have bank accounts with other banks. These are called nostro (to receive money) and vostro (to send money to) accounts.

The goal of the multinational to maximise their cash flow is the same common goal for banking customers. Unlike the SME, the multinationals have substantial influence over the banks. The cash flows can be the size of a country and therefore banks, especially the international ones, will tailor the services to meet the needs of that multinational. Services such as 'sweep accounts' that were created for the largest multinational clients are now widespread throughout banking, right down to individual accounts. SMEs can now use:

- Cash management modules (for pooling);
- FX systems –
    - Real-time market rates;
    - Trade execution;
    - Spot, forward and options.
    - E-banking (Internet systems).

The future

Banks want to be in this market as it provides them fee-based services and an ongoing revenue stream. Each bank, depending on its market, will provide one or more of the steps and usually has a correspondent bank in another country ready to assist in the process. The question has always been one of quality within the services offered. Unfortunately, banks thrive on inefficiencies and ineffectiveness when moving money. Banks immediately take the money and then, only over time, place in the the beneficiaries' accounts.

Banks need to and are increasing their margins. This is achieved through reducing cost and/or increasing revenue. The cost part is addressed by putting SMEs onto computer modelling and going digital, thus reducing the cost of people in the process. The revenue side is being addressed by charging for everything. Banking is a business and the perception of bankers being similar in stature to the medical profession and the clergy is changing.

Technology is starting to empower SMEs, as they can see how long the cash flow is taking and what fees are being extracted. With digital access, the choice of who does the banking has increased, as has who is providing the various banking services.

The regulators are starting to take charge of the process and eliminate poor practices from the banks. As they say, old habits die hard, and the banks, enjoying local regulations which makes opening a new bank very difficult, are like St. Augusta, who said: "Give me chastity and continence – but not yet".

CHAPTER 2

COMPLIANCE: NEW RULES AND REGULATIONS FOR BANK ACCOUNTS

Questions for SME directors

Do I need to:

- Perform basic due diligence on my customers, suppliers and banks?
- Be aware of Anti Money Laundering (AML) procedures?
- Employ a compliance officer?

Key considerations

- Banks are required to run checks and measures including Customer Due Diligence (CDD)/ Know Your customer (KYC) and enhanced due diligence (EDD);AML checks and measures including Customer Due Diligence (CDD)/ Know Your customer (KYC) and enhanced due diligence (EDD);
- US activities and their effect.

Compliance started in earnest in 2001

SINCE THE TERRORIST ATTACK on the New York World Trade Towers on 9/11 the US has led the world in trying to prevent the financing of terrorism. The initial legislation was focused in the Patriot Act, which defined regulations to prevent, detect and prosecute international money laundering and the financing of terrorism. The legislation included AML procedures and techniques that cover banking, finance and investment communities.

Applying enhanced due diligence includes:

- Establishing an AML program –
    - Appointing a compliance officer;
    - Procedures that are kept up to date;
    - Ongoing training;
    - Audit by a third party;
- Reporting suspicious activities;
- Verification of customer identity –
    - CDD/KYC – usual passport and proof of address;
- Due diligence on the people who own/control companies with shareholdings in excess of 25%;
- Confirmation of the sender and receiver of amounts in excess of $10,000 in cash;
- Confirmation of the authorisers of foreign bank accounts.

Ongoing AML

Worldwide legislation covering AML and counter-terrorism financing (CTF) is forcing banks and other relevant financial institutions and companies to ensure appropriate measures are in place to verify the identity of customers, track and report on suspicious matters, keep appropriate records and maintain rigorous internal AML/CTF programs. The increasing complexity of the legislation and particularly the 'ongoing' nature of it means that only the very smallest are able to do this manually without falling foul of the regulators, incurring large fines and suffering the resultant reputation damage that ensues.

The US Patriot Act has been replicated in many countries around the world. The World Compliance organisation (www.worldcompliance.com) reports over 100 countries have tightened their AML laws and placed greater emphasis on cooperation between countries.

This has led to the banking community being regulated and measured against how they are performing under the various in country regulatory authorities. In the UK, the Financial Services Authority (FSA) is due to be replaced by the Financial Conduct Authority for regulation in retail and wholesale markets for those firms not regulated by the Prudential Regulatory Authority (PRA), which will demerge from the FSA to be managed by the Bank of England. In the US, the regulators include the Federal Reserve and the Controller of the Currency. In addition, the US has passed two major pieces of regulation in the form of Sarbanes-Oxley (SOX) and Dodd-Frank, which have been designed to add protection and transparency to financial activities across companies and banks in the US. It is these regulators that decide who are fit and proper people to manage the banks and the penalties for non-compliance.

The Association of Financial Markets in Europe reported in October 2011 that:

- 50% of the banks performed inadequate EDD;
- 33% have ineffective procedures to indentify PEPS (see below);
- 33% have inadequate CDD;
- 33% have very high profits from areas where 'unacceptable' risk arises.

In fairness to the banking community, prior to the world going global, the opening of bank accounts required little research, as most of the people were local and known to the banking community there. Similarly, companies were locally based. Less than 30 years ago the actual information kept at the bank on a bank account was often minimal. Usually, just enough information is available to identify the owner of the account.

Politically Exposed Persons

Politically exposed persons (PEPs), their families and close associates are considered high risk and can be:

- A senior official in a country's administration, military or political party;
- A senior executive in a foreign government-owned company;
- A substantial owner of a company tied to a particular country;
- Any family members or known close personal or professional associates of the above.

The goal is to ensure funds going to and being sent by a PEP are above the law. World Compliance has created a database of 900,000 profiles of PEPs and average 25,000 new profiles and 5,000 updated profiles per month.

Due diligence by the SME

The onus on compliance with the various regulations lies with the financial institutions. However, it is necessary for the SME to know with whom they are dealing, not only from a compliance viewpoint but also from a credit point of view. Most companies provide and expect services and products to be paid for within 30 days. A company with a poor credit record or one which, when applying the bank's due diligence, flags up PEPs or connected directors to other companies which have had a record of poor business practice, may be one to keep a close watch on. It is wise to maintain an ongoing due diligence program.

Ongoing due diligence would include tracking the payments due against the relative strength of that particular customer. If the payments are getting later by the month and the company's credit record is deteriorating, then the necessary actions can be taken to ensure the potential damage is controllable. Similarly, if key directors who sign off the various activities change or are reported to or investigated by the authorities, care should be taken to protect the company's position.

Awareness of AML is needed especially if requests to pay away to third parties are made instead of to the company itself. Companies can contra payments and often do so when the customer is also a supplier. The payment owed is contra'd against the payment due (contra is Latin for 'against'). Again, contra against a third party needs to be considered carefully to ensure compliance in terms of AML and good corporate governance.

Due diligence of customers by the SME is a good practice. It helps understand the customer better and can prevent unexpected surprises.

Due diligence by the bank

Basic due diligence is information about the customer and the business relationship sought. The bank should have a clear idea of what the company is providing and what the business is about. Often, this is covered in the contacts between the bank and the company. Banks are obliged to verify the accuracy of the customer's explanation on the object and purpose of the company in order to establish the credibility and accuracy of the information.

Figure 2.1: Ongoing due diligence

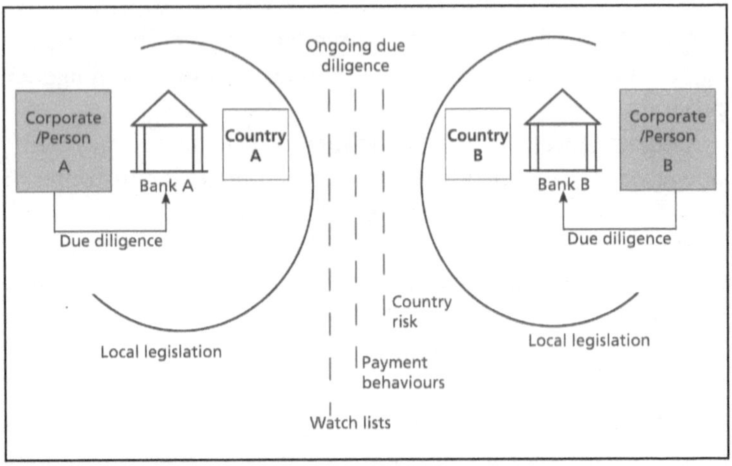

Source: Author

High risk criteria

- When data on the customer's identity is insufficient or not deemed to be reliable or accurate;
- When ambiguities for basic due diligence remain;
- When suspicions of money laundering or terrorism financing exist;
- When the business relationship includes transactions, services or products that may favour anonymity (e.g. use of cash);
- When the client is domiciled in, or transactions are carried out in, a country with a known record of encouraging terrorism.

In addition, extra due care is needed with a PEP who is resident abroad.

Documentation

The banks have found the easiest and quickest way to obtain information about the customer's identity and ownership structure is to ask the customer for the required information and documentation. The documents routinely requested are:

- A certified copy of registration certificate not older than three months;
- A certified copy of the share register – majority owners to undergo CDD/KYC – see below;
- A copy of the adopted business plan;
- A copy of adopted budget;
- The number of persons employed;
- All authorised signatures need to prove their ID and address (passport and utility bill).

The documents are checked for authenticity. The business plans are reviewed for logic, with heavy emphasis on cash flow. The people involved checked against watch lists and their credit records reviewed.

Customer Due Diligence/Know Your Customer

CDD/KYC is legally required by the banking community and is tracked by:

- Document management – the definition, scanning, management and tracking of customer documentation, and reporting of any deviations;
- Account monitoring – the tracking of movements over account(s) looking for deviations outside of a pre-determined profile;
- Watch list checking – watch lists are names of companies wanted by various governments. Enter a name and the system will check to see if the name, or like sounding names, appear on any of the watch lists (e.g. Office of Foreign Assets Control (OFAC), Bank of England and others). There is control over the granularity of the name checking so as not to create too many false alerts.

Messages that fail watch list checking are put to a quarantine queue for manual intervention;

- Message monitoring to check all inbound and outbound messages, irrespective of format, to see whether any field (normally the ordering customer and beneficiary) appears on one of the watch lists;
- Full audit trails of all checks and actions taken.

Anti Money Laundering

To establish a new bank account, the company needs to go through AML in addition to the bank's KYC requirements. These new requirements, coupled with Sarbanes-Oxley and Dodd-Frank in the US (financial and accounting disclosures), mean face-to-face meetings with the bank are often required. In addition, payments going out or coming into an account are screened against watch lists, as above. By law, the bank has to continually review payment transactions.

Under money laundering legislation there are essentially three obligations:

- To identify and verify customers (due diligence);
- To review transactions that could reasonably be expected to constitute or be aimed at money laundering;
- To report suspected cases of money laundering.

The purpose of the policy and the instructions are to ensure that the company's anti-money laundering and terrorist financing and other serious crime is always adequate, appropriate and in accordance with current standards.

Banks and credit companies are subject to criminal liability provisions of the law when they participate in certain financial transactions for one client. The new legislation provides for changes in a number of respects, including those relating to customer due diligence, providing information, compliance and enforcement. Money laundering legislation is important and difficult to apply as most legacy systems are not are designed to handle large amounts of data. Consequently, at many financial institutions procedures are layered across the existing infrastructure often in an electronic/manual way. The legal requirements must be observed by all concerned with or working with customers and money transactions for a company's business. It is important to work to prevent the company and its business being used for money laundering and terrorist financing and other serious crimes. To this end there has to be a constant awareness and ongoing checks to ensure payments being made are legitimate.

The Financial Action Task Force, FATF (Financial Action Task Force Against Money Laundering), was formed in 1989 by the G7 countries and is active. FATF currently has a mandate to continue its operations in 2012. The organisation publishes on its website information on money laundering and its activities (www.fatf-gafi.org). There are 40 recommendations forming the basis for much of the regulation concerning measures against money laundering, as well as updates to the lists of non-cooperative countries and territories (NCCT).

The money laundering schematic

Money laundering refers to measures taken to conceal or convert the proceeds of a crime, i.e. it is about action to 'launder black money white'. There is thus a prerequisite to ensure that money or other assets are not laundered profits from criminal activity.

Money laundering is usually schematically described as a process consisting of three stages:

1. Placement stage – the placement of money in a bank or a financial product;
2. Outline stage – transactions in order to break or hinder the links with the criminal origin;
3. Integration stage – money (or what has come in its place) is integrated into the legal economy.

Terrorist financing is usually considered as 'reverse money laundering', whereby profits from crime or other illegal actions are used to fund terrorist activities This means not only to make direct contributions to terrorism, but also to collect, provide or receive money or other assets to finance terrorism. The International Working Group on Financial Action Task Force (FATF) in October 2001 expanded its activities to include combating terrorist financing.

Risk-based assessment

Customer due diligence can be achieved by a risk-based assessment, the so-called 'risk-based' approach, which means that resources should be where they are most needed, i.e. in situations where the money laundering risk is greatest. Risk-based assessment is needed of factors such as who the customer is and what activities he engaged in, which kind of service / product the customer requires, the customer's residence and the countries in which transactions are carried out – some countries carry a much higher risk weighting than others.

Enhanced due diligence is required on transactions amounting to a sum equivalent to €15,000 or more.

Customer screening

Banks need to maintain an internal database of names that is automatically populated from publicly available lists such as OFAC, UN, EU, HM Treasury, DFAT and others. Many also maintains a 'bank's own approved list'. This list has been refined from previous activities of finding the system reporting a potential AML suspect being genuine. This is termed a false positive – that is, it looked like a positive hit on the watch list, only to find it was a like-sounding name. The bank list ensures that next time that client's payment passes straight through. For the purposes of automatic PEP list checking, interfaces with third party lists such World Compliance, Dow-Jones and others can be made.

Changes to the publicly available lists are automatically downloaded at a frequency defined by the user (normally daily). The changes will automatically update the bank's database and, if being used in an integrated manner, a complete sweep of the customer data repository will automatically be undertaken.

This ongoing sweeping (often termed extended due diligence, or EDD), say monthly, can help insure the integrity of the bank's customer base towards the established regulations. The established banks with millions of accounts have an enormous task in screening their older clients. Here many banks tend to be reactive to the customer when they request changes or additional services. At that request, the bank checks to see if the due diligence requirements are in place. If not then additional paperwork is requested. Often the expiry dates of passports are now tracked and upon expiry a new copy is requested.

Single view of the customer business within the bank (CRM)

Banks often struggle to maintain a single customer view of what products that customer has with them. The reason is a historic one. There are often many IT systems and business silos within a bank. Core banking systems (usually where the General Ledger is held) are often at least 10 years old. Updating of the modules tends to be a patchwork arrangement as replacing the core banking engine is both expensive and risky. Consequently, many banks' IT looks like solar systems, with information held based on the service needs rather than that of the customer.

Over the last few years many banks have installed Customer Relationship Management (CRM) systems, which collect data from the many systems. The information concerning a customer is then maintained only once, no matter how many branches the customer has a business relationship with. Similar from a compliance view, a director or beneficial owner can be viewed, no matter how many service offerings they have taken.

The amount of information that is now required, and continually is asked for by the regulators, is extensive. The data structure of older software needs to be revised, replaced or supplemented.

Account monitoring

Banks are continuously tracking customer accounts and linking multiple accounts from multiple host systems in a variety of combinations as follows:

- Aggregated, where many accounts in multiple host systems are pointed to one account and automatically analysed against a series of rules;
- One-to-one accounts are analysed against a series of rules;
- Mixed, where the user analyses host system accounts using a combination of aggregated and one-to-one accounts.

Bank applies compliance testing to bank accounts

To ensure compliance, banks have developed a series of tests that try to assess the chances of non-compliance taking place. These tests are often termed Business Intelligence (BI) rules. These set of rules track the bank account across three main categories:

- Turnover;
- Transactions;
- Behaviour.

Turnover rules are designed to monitor and flag abnormal changes concerning daily, monthly, rolling monthly and annual activities across value, type and number of transactions.

Transactional rules are where the bank defines the transaction types that are permitted and monitored over the account. For each transaction type, the bank can establish daily, monthly, rolling monthly and annual rules in respect of the value, number, type of transaction and geography.

Behaviour rules looks for sudden and arbitrary changes in the managing of the account. For example, the account suddenly goes from dormant to active. There are three basic activities that govern behaviour over an account:

- Entry point, which looks at the type and number of transactions conducted at more than one channel (branch, ATM, telephone, etc) within a given time period;
- Distribution that look at the type of transaction credited to an account and how the funds are dispersed over a user-defined time period;
- Dormancy rules, where the account is marked as dormant after a user-defined period of inactivity and reports it should the account become reactivated.

Bank applies compliance to payment messages

Banks are monitoring SWIFT and clearing payment requests using the screening tools on both inward and outward messages to check that the ordering customer, beneficiary bank, beneficiary customer or country are not on any sanction list stored in the database. Messages that are deemed suspicious are quarantined pending manual intervention.

Workflows ensure that, as a minimum, two people are involved in the releasing or suspending a message in the quarantined area. The reasons for the action taken on a message are recorded and held with the message. In the event that two clerical officers cannot agree an on how to process a message, it may be passed to a third person for final approval. For example, Santander puts such quarantine messages in a 'hold' queue; the hold reasons are investigated and resolved.

Additional regulation

The US and the EU are leading in producing new regulations to provide transparency across the financial chain. One such regulation, which is starting to overlap into each other jurisdiction, is Foreign Account Tax Compliance Act (FATCA). FATCA is aimed at US persons avoiding tax through the use of offshore accounts. Any US person who has money invested outside the US needs to report and comply with the Act.

The Act includes penalties for non-compliance. Starting July 2013 any financial institution with US customers will suffer 30% withholding on US income and capital payments unless the FI has established an agreement with the US tax authorities.

Heavy fines are levied against non-compliance by financial institutions by the in-country regulators. In the UK for example, the FSA fines in 2011 totalled £66 million.

The future

Banks are having to cope with an avalanche of new regulation to ensure that their clients are who they say they are, make certain that the clients are not funding terrorism or crime, keep a check on payment behaviour and notify the authorities if there are any such suspicions. This is a mammoth task, given most core banking systems are at least eight years old. The penalties for not complying will only grow. Most banks shrug off small fines as mere inconveniences or misunderstandings and address the situation only reluctantly. Regulators will continue to ensure best practices and compliance will not go back to the old days.

SMEs will also be assessed to who their customers are, and naivety will not be a defence. The leveller here is the Web, although it is full of both right and wrong information and needs to be checked when something seems out of character. It is also best to check with the client to see if any negative information is correct. It shows everyone the SME is switched on and cares.

SMEs can use the many social sites and research capacity of the Web to establish with whom they are dealing.

CHAPTER 3
BANK ACCOUNT STRUCTURES

Questions for SME directors

- Will our total bank balance be returned if the bank fails?
- Does our bank have a single view of our business and value us?
- Should we consider an alternative bank account structure?

Key considerations

- How many different banks should we use?
- Branch activities and the move to eBAM (Electronic Bank Account Management);
- Using client cash management accounts to manage the SME activities.

How safe is your bank balance?

MANY COUNTRIES offer deposit protection schemes, which pay out should the bank default. In Europe this tends to be about €100,000 per account per entity. Consequently, having more than €100,000 in an account carries the risk, should the bank default, that difference will be lost. Sweden, for example, is a country that has seen many of its banks disappear and many people there make certain that their money is spread across many banks.

In the US there is the Federal Deposit Insurance Corporation (FDIC), a government entity that guarantees the safety of deposits in member banks; each depositor is insured up to $250,000 per member bank. In 2006, The Federal Deposit Insurance Reform Act of 2005 (the Reform Act) was signed into law. The Reform Act merged the Bank Insurance Fund (BIF) and the Saving Association Insurance Fund (SAIF) into a new fund called the Deposit Insurance Fund (DIF). This change was made effective in 2006. In 2010, the Dodd-Frank Wall Street Reform and Consumer Protection Act (Dodd-Frank Act) was signed into law. The Dodd-Frank Act established a minimum designated reserve ratio (DRR) of 1.35% of estimated insured deposits, mandates that the FDIC adopt a restoration plan should the fund balance fall below 1.35%, and provides dividends to the industry should the fund balance exceed 1.50%.

According to JPMorgan Chase, the cost of the FDIC program is running at approximately 40 basis points per year. The FDIC has close to 1,000 banks on the watch list in terms of financial health. These banks are being monitored closely and often encouraged to merge to produce a fiscally stronger institution.

While bank accounts are often covered by insurance protection programs in case of bank default, usually up to $100,000 per account depending what money is in the account at the point of default, Credit Default Swaps (CDS) provide a payout equal to that which the CDS was prepared. Terms are usually in the $10–$20 million range and from 1 to 10 years, with five years being the average. The underlying documentation is provided by ISDA (International Swaps and Derivatives Association). A CDS is a credit instrument between two parties, which can be sold on in the market by either party.

Table 3.1: Deposit protection schemes

Country	Savings limit	Coverage
Belgium	EUR 100,000	100%
Bulgaria	EUR 100,000	100%
Czech Republic	EUR 100,000	100%
	Ordinary deposit guarantee scheme applies after September 30, 2010, covers up to	
Denmark	DKK750,000	100%
Finland	EUR 100,000	100%
France	EUR 100,000	100%
Germany	EUR 100,000	100%
Greece	EUR 100,000	100%
Hungary		
Ireland	Unlimited	
Italy	EUR 100,000	100%
Netherlands	EUR 100,000	100%
Poland	EUR 100,000	100%
Portugal	EUR 100,000	100%
Slovakia	Unlimited	100%
Slovenia	EUR 100,000	100%
Spain	EUR 100,000	100%
Sweden	EUR 100,000	100%
United Kingdom	GBP 85,000	100%

Stability ratings and stress tests

The FDIC assigns each financial institution into five categories. Composite ratings of 1 or 2 mean the institution is financially sound with only minor weaknesses. A rating of 3 means that if the weakness highlighted are not corrected, then serious financial distress could occur. A rating of 4 or 5 means substantial probability of potential loss.

The European Central Bank reported a financial stability review of the euro in December 2011 – a stress test on the eurozone financial system. The report highlighted several key issues:

- Contagion and negative feedback;
- Funding strains;
- Weakening local economies – credit risks for banks and a second round of funding needed;
- Imbalance of global economies.

The first point is a universal one. Once there is a common perception that a company, individual or country needs money, the more difficult it is to obtain it. It is important that perception does not overshadow reality, so communication is key in times of fiscal trouble. It is a question of confidence, so any stress testing results, if negative, should first be addressed in-house with a plan to correct the situation; then, if needed or legally required, the plan should be explained rationally to the media.

Bank account fees

Each bank has its own policies and charges surrounding the bank account. Many charge a monthly fee plus transaction charges. The fees become complex as they are often broken down by payment channel – cheque, ACH, wire transfers, cash – and charges added for incorrect usage of the account, e.g. payments being made with no funds in the bank. If there is no money or not enough money present when funds are requested, then no movement occurs and the bank reserves the right to charge for that failed transaction. Phrases like 'Insufficient funds' are used and the fees associated for rejecting items can be high. It is not unusual in the UK to be charged a £20 fee. In addition, for a direct debit to be returned, the beneficiary of the DD can also charge a fee, which too can be £20. These charges can be avoided by monitoring the cash flow though the account. Some banks offer a texting service, which shows their clients when the account is running low of funds.

Late payment fees are also high in the UK and there has been political pressure to lower them. Banks and credit card companies have responded that the fees tend to be £10–15 per item, as opposed to the £20–40 per item price range.

In addition, when a transaction has failed it is often reported to the credit bureaux. This in turn can lead to higher cost of credit or a decline in credit by banks as delinquencies result in poor credit scores. Once banks have declined credit, then those industries that specialise in higher risk situations come into play. Here credit maybe obtained, but the cost of it could be much higher than the bank.

In addition to fees, a bank may have policies regarding the handling of payments. The biggest one globally is the time allowed for crediting one account from another. Here it is in a bank's interest to make that time as long as possible. In Europe, SEPA aims to formalise the time banks hold the money by suggesting a three working day standard. The UK, for example, has a three-day ACH standard, with cheques returnable within 10 days. It is up to each country to set their standards and here value dating comes into effect (see below).

Most banks do not actually send an invoice for their charges, they simply deduct them from the account balance when due often with minimum information. These charges can add up and they often cover items which just appear without notice. This tends to be historic, for example, another bank adding a foreign exchange lifting charge and as it is money into the bank, the bank is reluctant to change. Hence a good relationship is needed with the bank to remove such charges as and when they occur.

Electronic Bank Account Management (eBAM)

Bank account management related to the opening, closing and maintaining of bank accounts is a manual, labour-intensive and often very slow process. It frequently involves paper-based transactions completed by visits to the bank with follow-ups by email, telephone, fax and mail.

These factors can contribute to high transactional and operational costs, inefficiencies, and a greater potential for fraud and exposure to risk.

eBAM is designed to remove the extensive paperwork required when opening and changing accounts at the bank. The process has been approved by the banking industry and is made up of 15 different eBAM XML ISO 20022 standard messages.

The eBAM solution is designed for existing customers only. It is for a customer that has an established relationship with the bank, or a new legal entity for a known customer. KYC requirements are not captured in the solution, as they should have been completed at time of the original bank opening. If any additional KYC activities are required they are handled as parallel and separate activities to eBAM.

The benefits of eBAM are:

- Single view of bank accounts;
- Bank-neutral solution;
- Reduces risk;
- Increases efficiency;
- Reduces operational costs;
- Achieves compliance.

Extensible Markup Language (XML)

To support eBAM the bank and the business have to be able to use Extensible Markup Language (XML) messaging. To illustrate how the 15 EBAM XML messages may be combined, we give here below three examples of business scenarios.

Figure 3.1: eBAM – opening a bank account

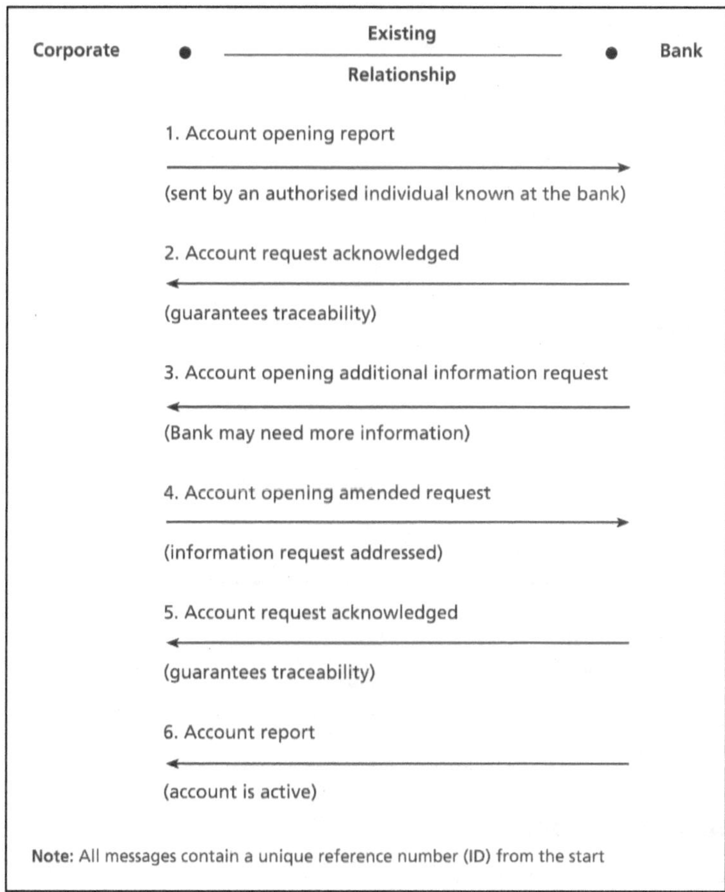

Source: Author

Figure 3.2: eBam – account maintenance

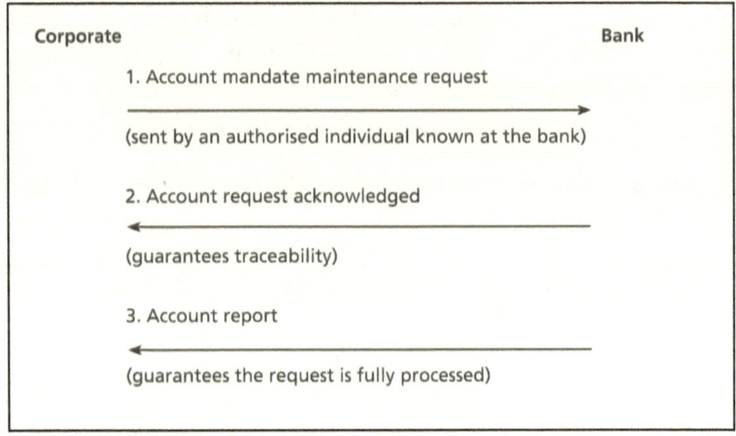

Source: Author

Figure 3.3: eBAM – account closure

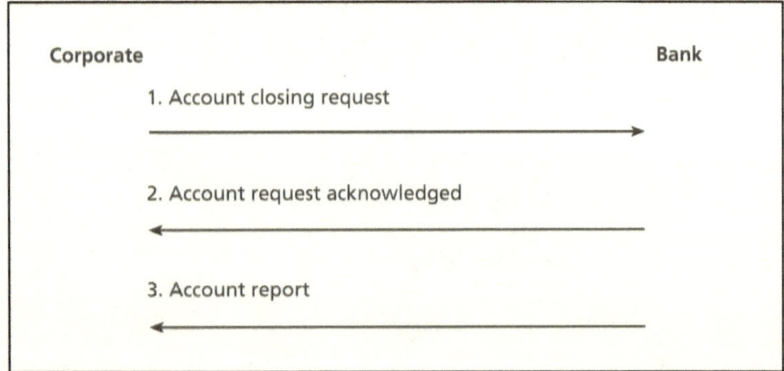

Source: Author

Banking mandates

Managing bank accounts involves the exchange of information on individuals authorised to perform financial transactions from the designated bank account(s). This information – commonly known as bank mandates - includes:

- Name;
- Function;
- Financial limits up to which one individual is authorised to order transactions;
- Financial limits up to which two individuals can authorise;
- Actual (physical) signature(s) of the individual on file.

Currently, this information is captured on paper on a 'signature card' and held at the bank. With the eBAM solution, the signature card is often not needed because the related information is within the XML message.

In addition, although the developed XML messages capture the core of the information needed to manage bank accounts, it is virtually impossible to replace the entire set of paper documents that is used today, due to the lack of harmonisation between/within banking groups; lack of harmonisation between countries/regions; and legal constraint based on each country's laws.

As a result, banks and businesses can complement the XML messages with these paper documents in electronic format. This data is attached as a file. In such cases these documents may often have to be digitally signed to comply with security requirements. Three business needs requiring digital signature at individual level have been identified:

1. Signatures of authorised individuals (e.g. CFO, Treasurer, Cash Manager);
2. Digital signature of the XML message containing the information on authorised individuals. This signature cans replace/complement the signature on the main mandate (the signature is that of the individual at corporate level);
3. Digital signature of an attachment to the XML message containing the non-standardised information and paper documents.

Message delivery can be sent over SWIFT. SWIFT's FileAct messaging service allows for electronic transportation of different items under different formats (XML + attachments in non- XML format) over SWIFTNet. Specific rules have been defined for the FileAct header info fields to enable transportation of eBAM-related information - XML and/or attachments.

Credit attached to the bank account

It is becoming common for a bank to attach an unsecured revolving line of credit to the bank account, which is called an overdraft. The bank sets the level of overdraft known as a credit line based on creditworthiness. However many banks now issue a small line – usually up to $500 to cover requests for money when the account is low. In many cases the cost of returning that request is often more than the request it self. A normal charge for an overdraft in the UK is 12–15% per annum. The charges are calculated and taken out of the account by the bank at the end of the month. If the amount being accepted by the bank exceeds the overdraft limit, then an unauthorised fee is charged. These fees are charged a premium rate for the amount of time the account has been in overdraft. These charges can be a factor of the country's base rate. For example, in the UK, an unauthorised overdraft can be many times the standard central bank rate, e.g. 30% against 0.5%. Authorised overdrafts in terms of revolving credit limit, interest rate levels and set-up and maintenance fees, are often negotiated between the bank and its client.

Bank accounts for third party cash administrators

The client cash account is centred on the 'other parties looking after your money' concept. The money has been transferred into an account, which only an authorised person, not the person who the money belongs to, can approve payments. These authorisers - companies - are called third party cash managers. Often found in many different business sector verticals, they may include insurers, solicitors, local authorities, rent collection agencies, pension administrators, trustees, internal banking for corporations, asset management, and broking.

The process is as follows. The third party operates like a bank, with the actual money staying in the bank. Cash receivables are collected from the business into one account. This account is reflected at the bank. The cash is then moved to accounts that can be set up instantly for cash to be paid out (accounts payable). The account holders can request payments and the administrator authorises the payment.

The need for third party cash management goes beyond the traditional commercial transaction-based activities. Increasingly, social factors are creating new groups of people who are generating burgeoning demand. One such group comprises the people suffering from dementia. Dementia UK noted in a report to the Alzheimer's Society in 2007 that there were then 700,000 people with dementia in the UK; this figure is expected to rise to over 1 million by 2025. Clearly, people suffering with dementia are likely to need third parties to handle their money. Another group comprises people who have a difficult time handling debt, which up to the crisis was freely available and plentiful.

Another group is those SMEs which would like some trusted persons to look after their money. Bankers used to be one of the most trusted professions after doctors and the clergy, but the financial crisis has taken its toll. In 2011 the Chicago Booth/Kellogg School Financial Trust Index noted only 23% of those surveyed said they trusted the US's financial systems, down from 25% in June 2011. A poll by Ipsos Mori for the BBC in the UK showed 70% of people had yet to restore their faith in banks now they had returned to profit. This leaves a very low level of confidence in the banks today.

The trusted third party can organise the cash flows by taking money at source – accounts receivable – then setting aside money to cover the regular commitments, and then paying away. Access to the account can be given to both parties so that they can see what has been paid and what is outstanding.

Client cash structure: today and tomorrow

Figure 3.4 provides an insight into the client cash relationships between the bank, the customer and the end clients. For each end client, the customer will have a ledger account opened on behalf of the end client. This is the conventional structure today for banks handling client cash using only a ledger-based solution.

The customer holds a single pooled account with the bank, which is an aggregate balance of the customer's client cash deposits with the bank. The end client's accounts are opened as virtual accounts and the total nets out with the total of the pooled account.

The virtual account model substantially reduces the number of bank ledger accounts and bank administrative resources required to operate a client cash service, whilst offering significant downstream customer benefits.

Figure 3.4: Virtual account model

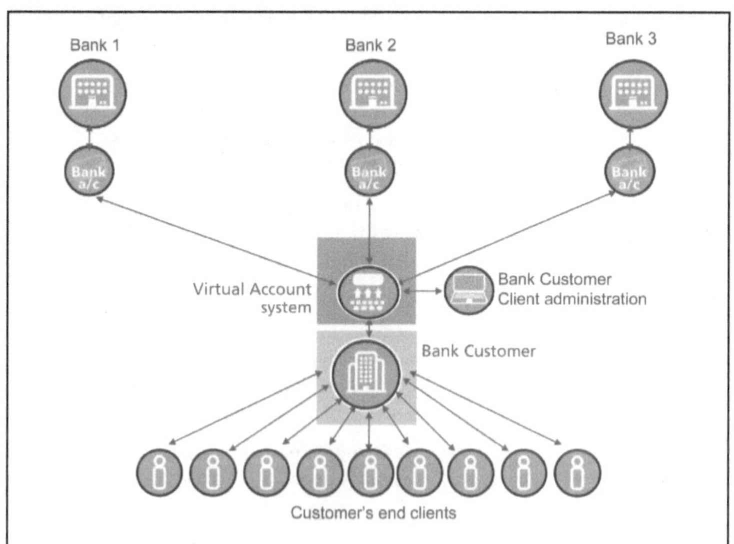

Source: Author

Benefits of client cash

The nature of the third party cash management business creates an extend chain of customers. Client cash offers a range of benefits for each of the customers in the extended customer value chain.

	Bank	• New business exploits scale economies of virtual accounts with minimal additional back office investment • Enhancement of capital adequacy positions (FSA and the Federal Reserve allows client cash to be counted as retail deposits) • Ability to offer different interest rates tied to certain accounts and the third party manager • Application of charges at account level • Bank branding
	Bank's customer	• Customer-friendly online access and control of virtual account structure • Near real-time client cash visibility across all accounts • Service efficiencies and administration cost savings requiring smaller back office • Customer's branding can be applied
	Bank customer's end client	• Access to near real-time information on individual accounts • Beneficiary of improved client service from reduced delay in the customer chain.

To illustrate the benefit, take the example of a conveyancing solicitor who is completing a house purchase for a client. With a ledger-based system banking system, a 'real' account is opened and managed by the bank on instructions from the solicitor (customer) on behalf of the house purchaser. Payments and receipts to the account are applied on the bank system with advice/confirmation by telephone and statements generated at the end of day. This convoluted situation is at its most acute when the home purchaser is awaiting confirmation of transfer of funds to the vendor to complete the property transaction. The customer experience is particularly poor, as multiple calls between the customer value chains are required, exponentially increasing the opportunity fees incurred by all parties.

Many of the global banks have developed bespoke solutions to service their client cash market. In essence, this top-tier group is able to take a long-term view of the market and so often will invest in developing a solution to meet their major clients' requirements.

The cost of in-house management of the multiple bank accounts held in the bank by the third party manager on behalf of their clients can be substantially reduced. For example, one of the largest UK property companies employs 10 people to simply reconcile the receipts and payments for rent, rates, insurance, cleaning and other services across their portfolio of properties.

Business employing third party accounts

Businesses can become third party managers for their own companies. The above structure can be layered across the existing bank account structure. The bank accounts feed the information into the third party's centralised structure. The central is then able to see where the money is located, and from the centralised pool (no actual money has moved), the third party manager can authorise transactions, resulting in subsidiaries receiving the cash as agreed.

The bank sees a reduction in bank accounts, often from at least 10 per third party to one. This saves on administration within the bank. One UK bank estimates it costs £80 per year to provide the infrastructure and support for a bank account. They also see a build-up of deposits as the money is pooled into one account from many, both within the bank and from other institutions.

The cost of a third party looking after other people's money is about the same as a packaged bank account, i.e. from £10 to £20 per month for active accounts, with inactive accounts often at a much lower level. The chief benefit from the payment side is that only payment instructions will be executed provided there are sufficient funds in the account.

The future

Most banks will continue to offer bank accounts and will not explicitly inform the holder if the account exceeds the insurance level. Others may notify you, although regulations for companies operating with other people's money are responsible for the money's safety. The chances are high that companies with client money under management will see a neutral third party holding the money and await their instructions. With today's technology the money can be moved virtually instantly and it does take away the temptation of another Lehman or GF Global using client's money for their own use.

SMEs will map their activities more closely to the information on the money themselves and make virtually instant payments. The tracking of the money will be in safe bank and non-bank warehouse accounts with known fees and conditions. These will be changed easily to reflect the improving banking infrastructure and the increasing digital age.

SMEs will have a minimum of two different banks working with them to avoid the fate of having everything in one basket. Banks themselves will encourage a secondary banking relationship providing, if they are the lead bank they retain 60% of the business transactions.

Banks will improve the billing process for SMEs, often under pressure from official groups, so fees become more transparent and easier to understand.

CHAPTER 4
LIQUIDITY MANAGEMENT AND CASH CUSHIONS

Questions for SME directors

- How big is our cash cushion in terms of operating expenses/months?
- Are our cash forecasts within 10% of the actual cash for the quarter?
- How liquid are our assets?
- What is the trend of our liquidity over the last 18 months and for the next three months?

Key considerations

- Maintaining liquidity is paramount;
- Banks' new capital requirements will affect everyone;
- Cash is king in times of economic uncertainty and stress;
- Knowing the degrees of asset liquidity.

Liquidity management

THE NEED TO STAY LIQUID is paramount. During these financially difficult times, banks are selling non-core assets to meet their regulatory obligations. Banks also need to manage intraday liquidity as they are receiving and paying out large amounts of money throughout the day.

While the trading floor often knows its actual cash position across assets within seconds, because of their size and complexity, banks often do not know. The best example of this was the Board of Royal Bank of Scotland, which when asked what its capital position was, noted that it ranged from 4% to 8% – a spread of billions of dollars, reflecting the complex nature of the business and a lack of internal coordination resulting in the inability to give an accurate figure to which it could be professionally managed.

Figure 4.1: Liquidity management for a bank

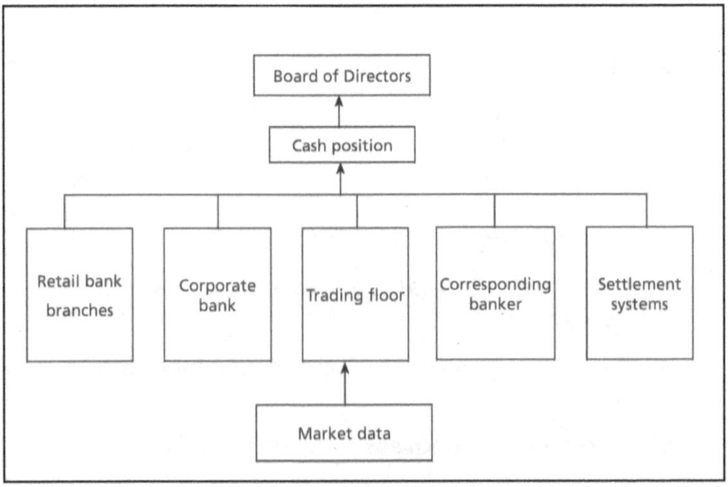

Source: Author

Liquidity management is the ability to pay bills when they become due over an acceptable time horizon, usually 12 months. Often companies have a three-month time detailed cash horizon and then a 12-month rolling average. Liquidity is now a main concern for everyone. Many check the balance on their bank account on a daily basis. This is becoming easier with e-banking and m-banking. Companies, up to and including Board members, are now requesting liquidity reports.

Reduction in bank lending capacity

The banks have been particular squeezed in this area over the last few years. The regulators are requiring banks to have more liquid assets (capital adequacy) to cover unexpected events. The term liquidity covers cash and cash-like financial instruments offered in the money markets, such as commercial papers (basically IOUs) and repos (a sale and repurchase agreement). Unfortunately, the credit crunch has seen a 'retreat to quality', making issuance for many banks at an acceptable rate of interest difficult.

The proposed Basel III is recommending a 15% capital adequacy ratio, as compared to Basel I, which was 8% for the smaller banks. Banks are allowed to lend money up to the level of the capital held back to cover unexpected events. Under Basel I the bank could lend a 12.5 multiple of the amount on deposit. By 2019, the multiplier will drop to 9.5, a reduction of close to 25% in lending terms. Also, the types of collateral that can be used is now greatly scrutinised and has to meet the 'Cash Outflows over 30-Day Stress Test', reducing the assets available for liquid collateral.

Table 4.1: Liquidation of balance sheet

Balance sheet item	Ready market	Up to 30 day risk factor	Over 30 day risk factor	
Fixed assets				
Plant/ Machinery	No	10%	50%	Asset Finance
Fixture/ Fittings	No	10%	25%	Asset Finance
Motors	Yes	75%	75%	
Current assets				
Inventory	Modern	50%	75%	Financing
	Historic	10%	25%	Financing
Cash	Yes	100%	100%	

Source: Author

To offset this reduction in lending capacity, banks have become very prudent over whom to lend to and often a review of their lending book to reduce exposure to sectors they believe require greater risk management. Consequently, the flow of credit funds has been reduced and the cost of these funds has increased. In addition, administration costs have risen as the level of due diligence has increased, both through new regulations and in terms of KYC and AML

Credit scoring

The main methodology of assessing credit is the use of credit scoring, and each bank scores credits in its own way. On the consumer side, outside agencies often score out of 1,000 points based on the use and repayment of credit. In the business market, the credit reports show the company's history, with many giving an indication of the creditworthiness at that point in time. These reports are only used as a guideline for banks in their own assessment of credit risk. The key to a good credit report is making payments on time, consistently. In addition, the most recent three months are of intense interest and any missed payments are regarded as very serious. Any blemishes in this period will overshadow the previous few years of credit history.

Degrees of liquidity

Assets held by a company should be graded by degrees of liquidity – i.e., the time it takes for the assets to be sold and converted to cash. Ownership of various items needs to be listed and an estimate of the time to convert cash made, forming a 'liquidity pyramid'. The same pyramid can be used with cash forming the base and non-liquid asset at the top. Every asset has a value and a time it would take to sell, either in part or whole. Owners of property can sell it completely, or take out some of the equity, or, if a company, sell and rent back the property. Each of these events causes cash to be raised. The timeframe can be six months to a year.

The higher up the assets are in the pyramid, the less liquid the company is. The loss of liquidity results in less flexibility being available to make decisions and take action. This is often referred to as 'mortgaging the future'. Control over highly illiquid assets is often lost and market forces tend to take over.

Cash and the flight to safety

The level of interest rate rises with the level of risk of the proposed investment. It is a balance between earning better interest rates and the chances of the return of the cash being extended. The bank is often prepared to pay more interest based on time and certainty of the money not being taken back. Consequently, the level of interest rises the longer the money is set aside. Also, terms and conditions surrounding longer-term money can result in bonuses and fines based on time. The bonus can be kept if the money is held another three months after term and extra amount of interest is received. The fines are applied if the money is taken out before the term, where normally no interest is paid. But the significant factor is: will the money be returned?

"Cash is king", as the saying goes, and as reported in CFO.com in December 2011, the latest report from REL Research shows public companies in the US continue to hold cash at record levels, with 1,000 of the largest companies holding $850 billion in cash. A further $800 billion is unnecessarily tied up in receivables, payables, and inventory. Company filings through June of 2011, shows that as revenues have increased over the past year, as has cash on hand, with companies now holding 11% more cash than they did in Q2 of 2010.

Total debt also increased by 7% during the period, indicating that companies are taking advantage of low-cost borrowing opportunities to increase their cash on hand. Companies are beginning to incrementally increase the amount of cash they are putting to use for purposes such as paying dividends, making capital expenditures, and share buy-backs. Companies are now taking 2% longer to collect from customers, and are holding nearly 2.5% more in inventory. Companies actually improved payables performance slightly, offsetting some of the losses in other areas.

It is a perpetual balance for a company between collecting the money in before having to pay it out. Most want the luxury of being paid immediately and then enjoy as much time as possible before paying out. In a zero-interest environment there is little to be gained by this practice, except the good feeling of having money in the account. It also provides a good track record to show the bank when going for credit. While some or all of it is required elsewhere, it does provide a sense of comfort, and often a false sense of confidence – beware!

The working capital numbers in the research clearly show that while companies managed to right-size their working capital in late 2009 in response to economic challenges, they lost focus once revenue growth returned, and the improvements made were not sustained. Companies become less efficient as accounts receivables grow, and they hold more inventory.

Cash cushions

Having cash in an account that is waiting to be paid away is not the same as a cash cushion. A cash cushion is designed to be able to handle events, both positive and negative, which demand immediate cash. The phrase 'saving for a rainy day' covers this behaviour. In the proposed Basel III regulations, a cushion of up to 2.5% is being promoted. Hence, in the event of an adverse change of business, the first 2.5% can be absorbed as business as normal.

The financial crisis has seen a change in behaviour towards money. Companies are holding cash with cash positions well above the 2007 levels. Going forward, the identification of a cash cushion should be determined. This way companies can see what they have as a fall-back position should difficulties arise.

Cash cushions should be considered a permanent feature and reviewed on a regular basis, say every six months. A level of 2.5% as for banking should be considered as measurement level for companies. Each company should clarify what that means financially. This analysis is often called stress-testing.

Stress testing

Stress testing supposes abnormal events that are plausible and comes this against the status quo. For example, how would a drop of 20% in revenue affect the ongoing solvency of the company? Similarly, how would a call from the bank to return 20% of the credit extended affects the future?

The future

Banks will end up capitalised to the requirements of Basel III by 2019. Many countries will insist on a higher capitalisation. In the UK, the Vickers Report is ring-fencing the banks' retail businesses from their investment and trading activities. The report recommends a capital ratio of 10% in risk-weighted assets (RWA) and a further 7–10% cushion to absorb any unexpected losses. That means that the UK retail bank will be capitalised at 17–20%.

Like the banks, SMEs will begin to report cash cushions. The availability of such reserves brings a level of confidence to shareholders, stock exchanges and regulatory bodies, as companies with cash cushions are showing prudence. The size of the cushion will be measured in terms of months of no money coming in, with 12 months as the target.

CHAPTER 5
PUTTING CASH TO WORK

Questions for SME directors

- Is our money earning any interest?
- How predictable is the stable money in the bank accounts?
- How can we get more certainty into our cash flow?
- Have we done a stress test on the cash flow?

Key considerations

- How to put cash to work effectively;
- Islamic banking;
- Interest rate forecasts;
- Taking advantages of stable balances.

Earning interest

Most banks recognise the need to provide a return on the balances in an account. The birth of the NOW account in the US recognised this need and banks offered accounts with perpetual interest being applied to any balances. Interest is dependent on the country; for example, France does not permit interest to be earned on certain bank accounts. Islamic banks, as an example, do not permit interest at all.

Islamic banking

The Institute of Islamic Banking and Insurance (www.islamic-banking.com) states: "Islamic banking refers to a system of banking or banking activity that is consistent with the principles of the Shari'ah (Islamic rulings) and its practical application through the development of Islamic economics". The principles, which emphasise moral and ethical values in all dealings, have wide universal appeal. Shari'ah prohibits the payment or acceptance of interest charges (riba) for the lending and accepting of money, as well as carrying out trade and other activities that provide goods or services considered contrary to its principles. While these principles were used as the basis for a flourishing economy in earlier times, it is only in the late 20th century that a number of Islamic banks were formed to provide an alternative basis to Muslims, although Islamic banking is not restricted to Muslims.

Islamic banking has the same purpose as conventional banking except that it operates in accordance with the rules of Shari'ah, known as Fiqh al-Muamalat (Islamic rules on transactions). Islamic banking activities must be practiced consistent with the Shari'ah and its practical application through the development of Islamic economics. Many of these principles upon which Islamic banking is based have been commonly accepted all over the world, for centuries rather than decades. These principles are not new, but arguably, their original state has been altered over the centuries.

Islamic banking does allow fees to be charged. This is transparent when buying and selling goods for cash and Islamic banking works well. The fee for activities for which interest is used needs to be redefined as a fee, which meets the needs for an Islamic customer. Here new Islamic methods of finance have been developed which were approved by a recognised Islamic scholar. Cash management is as important in the Islamic world as it is elsewhere.

The ability to move cash instantly removes a number of barriers for Islamic banking. For example, having same-day FX removes the need to fund the two-day wait for one of the currency pairs to arrive. Both currency payments occur at the same time, meeting Islamic requirements on completing a commercial obligation there and then.

Linking the savings module to the bank account

The most common is the linking of a savings module to the bank account. The two accounts often have different numbers and are kept separate from each other. The company can manage the funds in either account by instructing the bank to move the money between the two. Often, should the bank account go overdrawn, the savings account remains as is unless the bank has an automated system and agreement with the business to move the money between the separate accounts. Overdraft charges tend to sharply overshadow the level of interest the bank is prepared to pay on a savings account.

Figure 5.1: Bank account with savings account

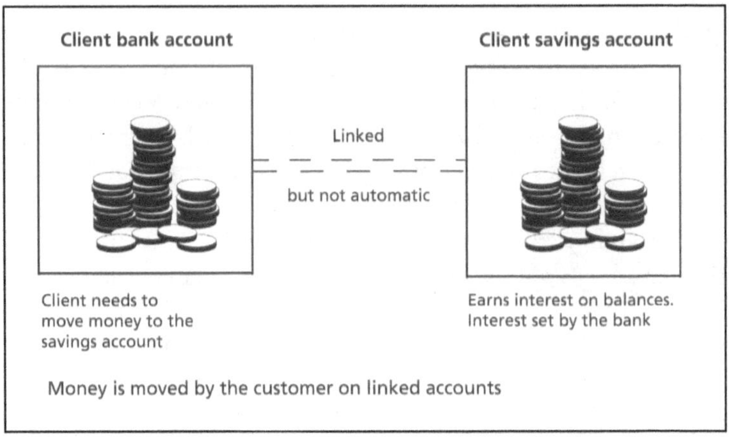

Client bank account

Client savings account

Linked

but not automatic

Client needs to move money to the savings account

Earns interest on balances. Interest set by the bank

Money is moved by the customer on linked accounts

Source: IBS Publishing

Outside investments

As the balances in the main account grow, some banks have the option to move money into higher interest paying accounts outside the bank offerings. To take advantage of these accounts, the minimum amounts being moved start at $25,000 increments. Depending on the bank, the number of outside investments can be high, with a wide variety of risk available. The level of risk is clearly indicated and the business is advised of its nature. These outside the bank investments have lead to many businesses having an investment policy on the level of risk being undertaken. There is a hierarchy of risk levels, especially in bonds, which start with ratings by the major agencies from A+ downwards. Outside of bonds, money market and commercial paper, few businesses invest elsewhere, with virtually none in equities.

Figure 5.2: Outside investments

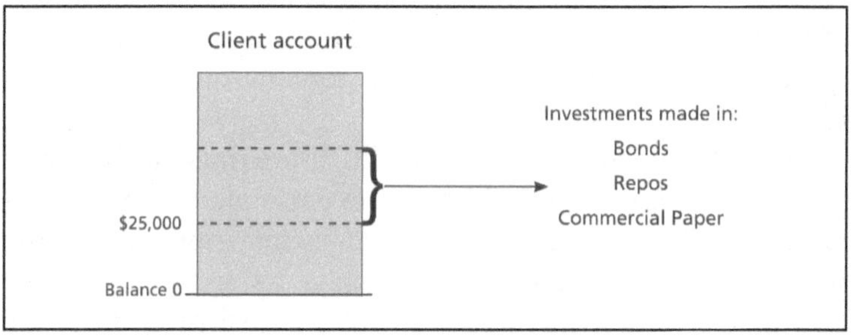

Client account

$25,000

Balance 0

Investments made in:
Bonds
Repos
Commercial Paper

Source: Author

Forecasting cash flows

Over time the pattern of money flowing into the bank account becomes predictable. Often a company has peaks and ebbs in its accounts. The account can be reviewed to see which monies can be invested for a longer period. Banks often pay more interest on monies put on deposit for longer times. Hence, businesses with established balances can earn more money by moving day-to-day savings into longer-term commitment – seven or 30 days or three or six months.

Figure 5.3: Company balance over time

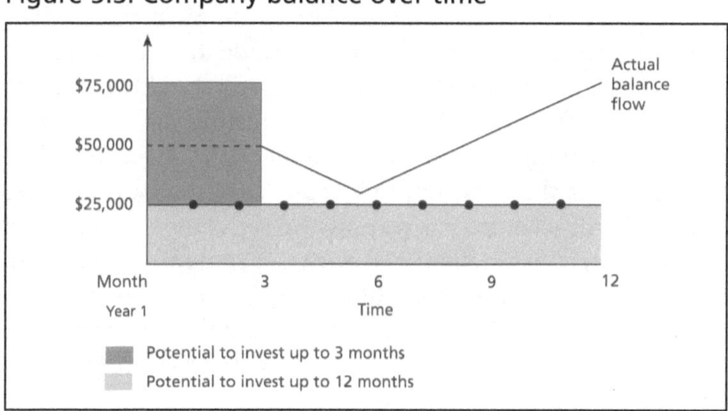

Source: Author

The area of forecasting money both into and out of the account has received little attention to date. Most banks do not offer any services around this area of cash management.

Businesses are also guilty of not forecasting cash flow for accuracy.

The entire need for forecasting the future financial health of the company is changing. In the US in particular, the Sarbanes-Oxley (SOX) legislation, asks directors for comment on the future. The Australian Stock Exchange as another example also requires companies with a negative cash position to file accounts showing estimated cash flows over the next quarter. The goal for regulators is to create an early warning system to help prevent major corporate disasters such as Enron and Worldcorp and financial institutions such as Lehmann Brothers and MF Global. The forecasting discipline being demanded by the regulators can also be helpful to banks and businesses.

Predicting revenue and expenses

The keys for generating a cash forecast are revenue and expenses. The expenses side tends to be the easier of the two to predict. Most companies' costs lie in people. Given many countries' employment laws, these costs, depending on the length of service the people have with the firm, should be considered with a minimum of three months' break. In most cases, when layoffs are required there is money set aside to meet the financial redundancy needs. However, the payroll should be forecast as it is today for the next 12 months, adjusting each quarter to the changes in the company head count.

Revenue is the most unpredictable, as is the cash arriving into the bank account. It is common to see company financials on a quarterly basis compared with the same time period 12 months prior. While proceeding through the financial year, the half year should be compared to the half year 12 months prior, and, similarly, the 3rd quarter compared to its prior year's counterpart. Similar cash flows should be forecasted. In this way, the next quarter's cash and 12-month rolling forecast can be reviewed and actions made to improve the cash collection and to make determinations on the cash distribution. In addition, the business can foresee potential shortages or excesses

The revenue component can be split into two – recurring revenue and all other. Recurring revenue is common in many sectors, for example insurance and software. Here clients have agreed to pay monthly or quarterly revenues tied to signed contracts. (The best contracts are those that exceed three years or more as they can be securitised and used as collateral should additional funds be required). Most companies have a combination of the two. The next step is to turn this into predictable cash. The best way to do this is to sign up a direct debit (DD). Not only does this make the cash 95% predictable, it also guarantees the cash will arrive on a certain date.

A few banks are starting to work with businesses in assisting them in forecasting the cash needed over the next four quarters. This is initially being done with the larger or more visionary institutes. Forecasting does change the relationship, with one Japanese bank pointing out their intention of a joint plan so as to become more intimate with their clients. The IBM Institution of Banking for Business Values in Banking report 'Fit, focused and ready to fight' echoed the Japanese view that 'customer intimacy will generate client loyalty'.

Figure 5.4: Forecasting company balances going forward (1)

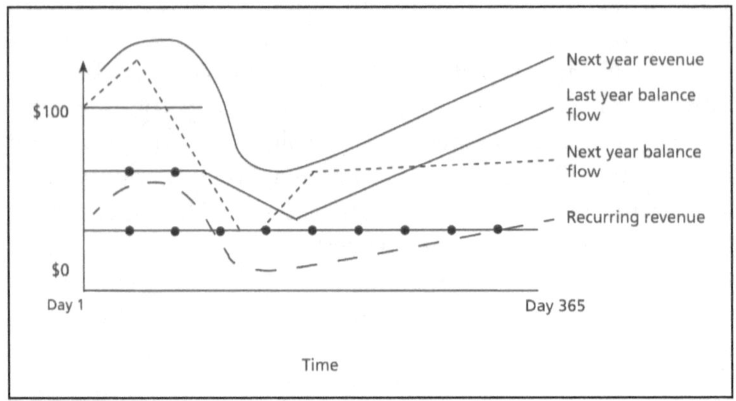

Source: Author

Figure 5.5: Forecasting company balances going forward (2)

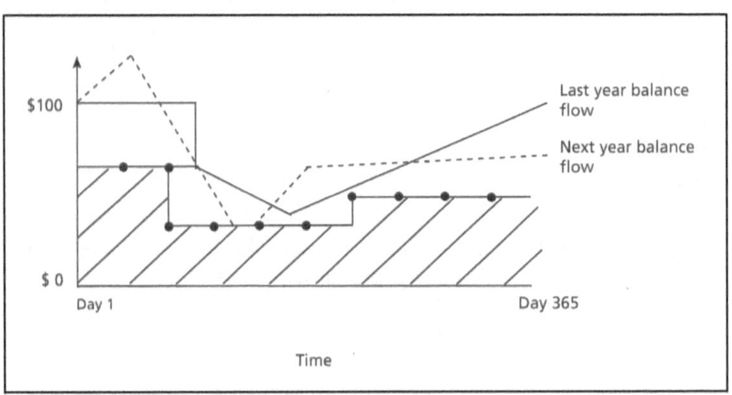

Source: Author

Making money on the money

The worldwide environment for interest is based on the level of risk of the instrument taking the money. The safest investment in which the principal is guaranteed to be returned is offered by the banks themselves, with insurance protection programs.

The rates the banks are offering are very low and could stay that way for the next few years. Most economic forecasts are similar to the Wells Fargo example below:

Table 5.1: Wells Fargo economic forecast 2011

Country		**GDP**	
	2011	**2012**	**2013**
Global	3.50%	3.20%	3.70%
Advanced Economies	1.50%	1.50%	2.10%
Developing Economies	5.90%	5.30%	5.70%
USA	1.70%	1.50%	2.10%
Eurozone	1.50%	2.00%	1.90%
UK	0.90%	0.80%	1.70%
China	9.20%	8.20%	8.60%
India	7.30%	7.10%	7.70%
		3 Month LIBOR	
Interest rates	**2011**	**2012**	**2013**
US	0.50%	0.50%	0.45%
Japan	0.20%	0.20%	0.20%
UK	1.00%	0.70%	0.70%
Eurozone	1.20%	0.70%	0.70%
		10 Year Bonds	
Interest rates	**2011**	**2012**	**2013**
US	2.10%	2.50%	2.60%
Japan	1.05%	1.15%	1.16%
UK	2.40%	2.70%	3.00%
Eurozone	2.20%	2.60%	2.80%

As central bank interest rates have fallen to the lowest level in recorded history (for example, the Bank of England rate is currently 0.5%), to help prevent an economic depression the interest rates offered by the banks themselves have also fallen. Historically, banks are the first to drop interest rates when the central bank lowers its banking rate, but often lag when the interest rate rises. An increase in the bank interest rate gives the commercial banks a window of opportunity (usually four to six weeks) to increase the spread between the cost of the money to the bank (interest paid out) and the money they earn on loans.

The central bank rate is the basis of rates charged to those banks borrowing from them. Each country has its own central bank looking after that country's currency.

Given the current global economic situation, the GDP of the advanced economies is expected to grow 1.5–2%, while the developing economies' estimated growth is 5–6%. In other words, the developing countries are expected to grow three times faster than the advanced ones, as is made clearly evident by the rise of the economies of China and India.

The interest rates now being offered by banks for immediate use of money is extremely low, often 0.01%. These rates climb based on agreements involving the length of time money is put into the market (for example time deposits) and amount. See Figure 5.6.

Figure 5.6: Interest rates vs. time (UK, December 2011)

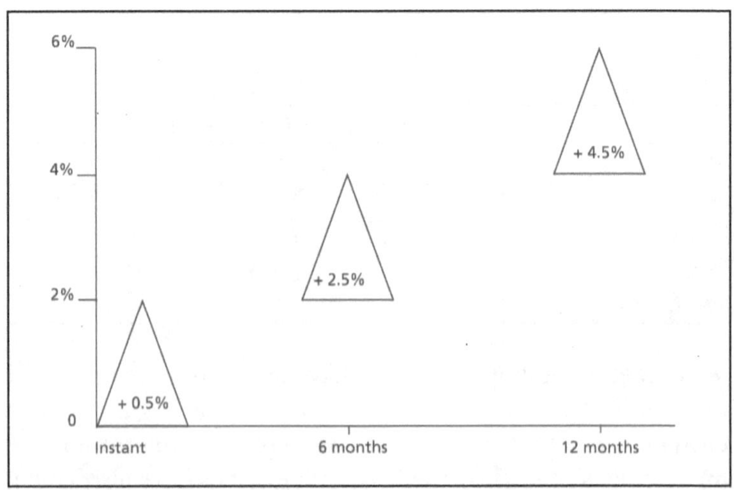

Source: Author

The future

It is highly likely that interest rates will remain low for a while, so cash has to work hard to earn any money. The banks are highly unlikely to offer any where near market rates, especially to existing customers. The phrase 'for new customers only' reflects greater returns to new rather than existing clients. For a bank, the cost of the interest reduces their margins.

SMEs need to continually review where the best interest rates are being offered. These rates may not be from banks, so security and confidence in getting bank 100% of the money is needed. For Islamic businesses with surplus cash, interest is forbidden. Holding that surplus in a strong currency may appreciate the cash without interest.

CHAPTER 6
RISK AND INTEREST STRUCTURES

Questions for SME directors

- Should keeping surplus cash in a stronger currency than the home currency be considered?
- Is there an investment strategy for cash over the short and medium term?
- Is gold with a stop-loss as an investment worth considering?

Key considerations

- Understanding risk levels of investment from safe to speculative;
- Using currency and gold as an appreciating cash asset with stop-losses;
- Gold trends.

The investment risk pyramid

The level of interest being paid for cash is proportional to the risk of the instrument and the issuing organisation. The instruments are often rated by the agencies, as they are seen in the market as being unbiased. The investment pyramid that follows shows the base as being 100% safe, rising to highly speculative. Most Cash Managers invest the cash-in-hand at the base level. It is convenient and safe, but barely keeps up with inflation in most countries.

Figure 6.1: The investment pyramid

	Risk	Liquidity
Derivatives - mark to market - hedging	50% to 100%	3 to 5 days
Appreciating cash investments - strong currency - gold	Stop-loss 15%	3 to 5 days
Cash in account	Fully safe	1 to 3 days

Source: Author

Base level investments – no risk to principal and highly liquid

This is a set of ultra-safe investments that, as a result of these fiscal depressed times, paying minimal interest rates (e.g. in the UK less than 3%):

- Cash deposits in the bank account – 100% liquidity and money available within three days. Accounts secured up to €100,000 in case of default;
- Bank may offer greater interest on the account by increasing amount size;

- Cash sent out to money market funds (money is returned after an agreed timeframe – 30, 60, 90, 120 days – usually with minimum amounts of £25,000);
- Repo agreements (minimum amount of £25,000);
- Commercial paper (minimum amount of $100,000).

In Sweden the authorities have allowed a special deposit taking licence to be given to certain companies that can provide the security necessary to cover the deposits should they default. The authorities keep a watch on these companies to ensure the savings are protected as best as possible. The authorities can stop or restrict the level of deposits being taken if their analysis and stress testing suggests the company is potentially in trouble. The authorities insist that an individual can only invest up to £5,000. These accounts are currently paying 6% for money up to a year and 5% on a day a to day basis. The bank insurance program does not cover these deposit offerings.

SMEs can invest much more than the individual. The authorities view SMEs as being financially sophisticated and as such can put in as much money as they like. Most countries have a sophistication test for the individual. Basically, a person signs a statement to say that they are well aware of the issues investing out of the safety of the banking structure and accept the risk. The risk is usually spelt out in the statement and covers the worst possible outcome – the loss of all the money.

Appreciating cash investments – up to 15% market risk and highly liquid

As there is little money to earn on base level instruments, companies can hold assets which are highly liquid and can appreciate above a level of potential forecasted loss. By taking a known and approved risk (for example a stop-loss at 15% below the market price at purchase), strong gains can be realised over the short to medium term.

A stop-loss order is an instruction to sell the currency (or any security, including gold and bonds) when the market price falls below the purchase price. For example £10,000 is converted from GBP to USD. The conversion rate is 1.58, so $15,800 is the amount held in dollars. The level of risk taken is based on a company's own assessment. The maximum loss suggested is 15%. A stop-loss is requested such that when the price of the dollar reached 1.85 then the currency is sold. At 1.85 the amount of pounds being repatriated is £8,540. The loss has occurred because the USD has weakened against the GBP. Consequently more dollars are needed to buy pounds. This is true for all market-traded securities, currencies and commodities.

These investments are as follows.

A strong currency

The cash is deposited in a particular currency other than the one the company is currently operating in. The currencies have to be monitored and a level of loss attached to the investment. For example, the currency normally is GBP and the cash is parked in Chinese Renminbi (RMB). Should the RMB to GBP exchange rate drop by 15% (or the level of loss agreed), then the Chinese currency is converted back into pounds. In the last two years the RMB has appreciated 16% against the euro. The cash in the adopted currency can use the same base level investments as above, with the exception of agreed timeframes. The timeframes restrict the movement of the currency and open it up to market risk. Liquidity into cash can be quick, with payment being made usually within three days.

Gold

The cash is deposited into gold. Gold has appreciated consistently over the last five years. In 2011, gold rose 12% year-on-year. Again, a level of market risk has to be assigned and the gold price tracked, with a stop-loss of less than 15% of the price purchased. While there is no interest rate opportunities for the gold but it can be used for collateral for securing credit. Using gold as collateral can reduce the speed of liquidity, thus exposing it to more market risk than agreed. Liquidity into cash is fast, with payments made usually within three days.

The commissions for buying and selling the currencies and gold should be factored into the risk level before moving into appreciating cash investments. The longer-term cash cushion could be invested into these alternative cash funds.

Speculation – up to 50% market risk

Derivatives are in this category as they can be used for hedging and high-risk investment. In this category spread betting can be added, along with options, futures, warrants, swaps and contracts for difference (CFDs).

Speculative investments using derivatives can:

- Make a greater gain or loss from the same price movement that would result in actually buying the underlying asset in the first place;
- Make a gain from a fall in the price of the underlying asset.

Gold – the universal currency

Gold can be described as a universal currency. It is often held by central banks, and in 2009 the Indian central bank bought 200 tonnes from the IMF (International Monetary Fund).

Gold used to play a central role in the international monetary system until the ending of the Bretton Woods system of fixed exchange rates in 1973. Since then, the role of gold has reduced, although it is still an important asset in the reserves held in by many countries. The IMF is one of the largest holders of gold in the world. As of 31 August 2011, the IMF's gold was worth $164 billion.

Gold is a finite resource and used in many applications as it does not rust. Most gold comes from South Africa; since

1910 75% of all gold ever produced has been extracted there. It is estimated that all the gold in the world that has ever been refined would form a cube 20 x 20 x 20 metres.

Similar to FX, the price of gold is readily available and relatively easy to convert into cash. The price of gold is fixed twice a day and this forms the basis of the price of gold offered in the market. Gold is priced in USD per troy ounce (31.1 grams; one ounce equals 24 carats). The price of gold is pro-rated to the number of carats used in its make-up. The popular amounts are 22, 14 and 9 carat gold.

As gold is priced in USD, a UK entity would have seen the value of gold increase consistently over the last five years. Since 2008, the price of gold in sterling terms has increased 34%, 13% and 31% in 2010. In 2011 it rose 12%.

When buying gold bullion the price is based on the amount being bought. For example, buying one-ounce gold coins can carry a 10% spread over the fixed rate at that time. By buying 100 coins the price drops to around a 7% spread.

Figure 6.2: Gold – London PM Fix 2000-2011

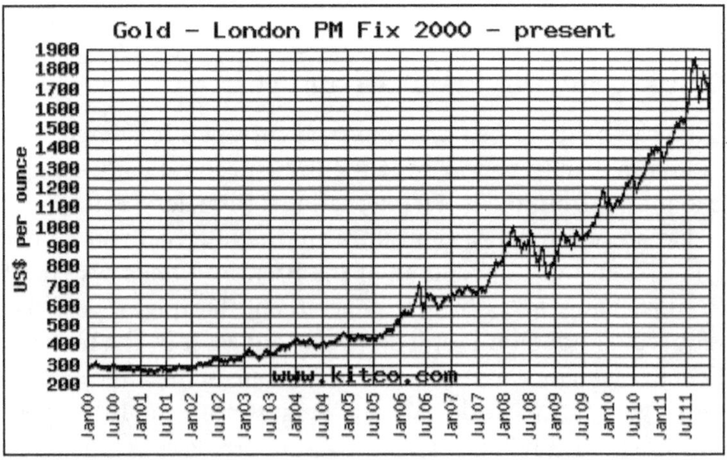

Source: www.kitco.com

The future

Probably the first question any SME should ask concerns their home currency – is it strong? Many companies in countries with weak currencies, for example Zimbabwe, hold deposits in USD and euro regardless of the interest rates being paid in their home country. In the future, the Chinese currency, the Renminbi, could well join these two world accepted currencies, given the economic growth of China.

Banks view individuals' deposits as stable. Deutsche Bank estimates that 40 to 60% of the revenue from payments comes from NII (net interest income). For the individual, the reward is a very low rate of interest. Part of the issue is the inertia of going to the bank and moving the money. Now with technology, money can be moved instantly, into both banks and non-banks that are offering a higher rate of interest. Most of the time a monthly term (a 28-day tie-up) is sufficient for cash flow and a higher rate of interest.

It is more than likely that interest rates will increase as the economy improves. In the meantime the the European Central Bank has lent 800 European banks €529 billion money with an annual return of 1%. These loans are due to be paid back after three years, when hopefully growth has returned to the economy.

A number of investors are recommending a portion of cash be put into gold. Like currencies, gold is readily liquid. Web technology helps buy, sell and monitor assets.

CHAPTER 7
THE CREDIT LADDER

Questions for SME directors

- What is your average cost of credit today and how does that compare to last year?
- Do you have access to credit at a good interest rate, should you need it?
- Who is managing the credit rating displayed by outside agencies?
- Has anyone provided personal guarantees?

Key considerations

- Watch out for credit facilities charges;
- Credit agencies are monitoring trading activities.

Charges for credit facilities

SMEs ARE FINDING it difficult to access credit from banks at this time and the cost of borrowing has increased. The spreads - interest rates - offered by banks and specialised lenders have grown dramatically. The key is the annual percentage rate (APR); the greater the figure, the more interest is being charged and the more money is needed to pay back the credit. In addition, there could well be additional fees for setting up the credit, including administration charges as well as penalties for paying back early.

Table 7.1: Charges for credit facilities

Type of credit facility	Term	Collateral	APR
Corporate loan	3–5 years	Sometimes required	5–10%
Account overdraft	Ongoing	No	10–18%
Credit cards	Ongoing	No	10–35%
Invoice financing	4–6 weeks	Yes	18–36%
Unauthorised account overdraft	Ongoing	No	18–36%

Source: Author

The cost of credit is determined by the credit rating, the amount needed and how quickly the money is needed. One area that has come to the front in difficult financial times is the payday loan. The cost of borrowing £400 for 28 days can cost £100-£150. At the end of 28 days the money is either repaid or rolled over. Within three months, the interest costs equal the original loan. Most countries do not regulate the cost of such loans; therefore, providing you are over 18, the sky really is the limit for the interest rate.

UK banks are encouraging SMEs to move from revolving credit to invoice financing. For the banks it exchanges ongoing unsecured credit for collateralised time-sensitive credit, and at a higher interest level. The change-over occurs as the bank requests a reduction in the credit line, which under its terms and conditions it is legally entitled to do. As the reduction is often 30-50%, the need for credit is necessary and the SME has often little choice, especially if it is tied to one bank.

Table 7.2: The credit ladder

Interest rate	Type of credit	Term	Collateralised
0 to 10%	Corporate loan	3 to 5 years	Possibly
	Leases	3 to 5 years	Yes
10% to 20%	Revolving credit - overdraft on accounts - credit cards	Ongoing	No
20% to 30%	Invoice financing	4 to 6 weeks	Yes
	Authorised overdraft	Ongoing	No

Source: Author

Credit rating agencies

On the country and corporate front there are three main credit agencies: Fitch, Moody's and S&P (Standard and Poor's). Their mission is to establish the likelihood of a default on monies being advanced. While they have different credit analysis techniques, the end-result of a league table from AAA to Ca rating is similar. The greater the chances of being repaid, the higher up the table the country or company is positioned. Here, for Fitch and S&P, AAA is the highest credit rating that can be achieved, while Aaa is the Moody's equivalent. These ratings are regarded as 'Prime'.

For a Prime rating, a borrower would see very low rates of interest and readily available, as the chances of default are minimal. The term 'flight to quality' covers the movement of money out of lower rated credit instruments to those of a higher quality, especially Prime. In difficult financial times the cost of money for Prime customers can actually go down, such is the demand. Hence the economic and prestige value of being Prime is very attractive.

The price and availability of credit below AAA is dependent on the market. In times of crisis, credit availability dries up and what is available commands high prices and shorter durations.

Table 7.3: Credit rating agencies ratings guide

Credit category	**Fitch/S&P**	**Moody's**
Prime	AAA	Aaa
High Grade	AA+	Aa1
	AA-	Aa3
Upper Medium Grade	A	A1
	A-	A3
Lower Medium Grade	BBB+	Baa1
	BBB-	Baa3
Non-investment Grade	BB+	Ba1
	BB	Ba2
Substantial Risks	CCC	Caa
Extremely speculative	CC	Ca

Source: Author

The grade of BB+ and below is regarded as 'junk' in the market. The lower the grade, the less chance there is of100% of the principle being returned. If a client is rated as junk, it often results in a proposed 'haircut' to help keep the client solvent. A haircut is the establishment of a price that is below the original valuation of the asset. The euro crisis has seen Greece being downgraded between CCC and Ca by the three rating agencies, and many owners of Greece's debt have taken a 50% haircut. That is, if they had put £100 million into Greece's sovereign debt, then only £50 million will be returned.

Initially, the feeling in the market was the euro could be credit rated as a whole rather than by individual country. The early ratings were as a group and market sentiment backed that view. This was similar to Citibank's view that countries do not go bankrupt (held before the Latin American debt crisis). Now each EU country is judged on its own fiscal resources. To return to group ratings, the European Central Bank would have to be the lender of the last resort for all of the European debt. This is difficult, as the amount of debt is in trillions and politically there needs to be a way of preventing excesses across the group. The European banks themselves have taken €489 billion in loans in 2011. This followed €300 billion of loans in 2009. In 2012, the European banks need to refinance €700 billion as existing contracts mature. The interest rate on the €489 billion was 1%.

Credit reports

Credit reports for SMEs and consumers are available in many countries. These reports are similar in intent to the credit rating agencies; they give a prediction on the likelihood of the money being repaid on time and in full. The three leading credit reference agencies in the UK are Equifax, Experian and Callpoint (US partner of Transunion). In the US, the credit agencies are called credit bureaux and the same three in the UK are joined by Innovis as US market leaders.

The credit companies offer a credit score per person. Most score out of 1,000 from a list of items that include:

- Stability of the entity;
- Number of financial accounts;
- Colour coding of the performance against those financial accounts, for example:
    - Green – payments up to date
    - Yellow – payments 1 to 3 months late
    - Red – payments 4 to 6 months late
    - Black – Default.

Most of the agencies include a search for identity fraud and report if such frauds are found. They also provide access to the credit report file for a monthly fee. For companies, the report can be purchased by anyone.

The higher the credit scores, the better chance of being approved for credit by financial institutions at reasonable interest rates. The lower the credit score, the less likely credit will be extended and less likely the SME is to receive the advertised level of interest.

Banks and financial institutions' scoring techniques

Banks and financial institutions have their own scoring techniques. These are developed to reflect the level of risk they feel comfortable with at the time. These scores can be moved up or down depending on the credit appetite of the institution. Credit appetite is a measurement and desire that refers to the amount of credit that financial institutions want to extend to a particular market segment or group of companies or type of loan. In times of crisis, the appetite is often reduced and as such, the higher credit scorers are approached first for any approval. In the UK, for example, the level of property investments made by banks in the past now severely restricts new bank money being allocated and approved for this sector.

After working with a company for a while, banks are usually open to reviewing the credit facilities available. These credit facilities tend to start with an overdraft facility, an easy first step for the business and the bank, to cover cash transactions during the month. Bank credit reviews are carefully performed, as overdraft credit is an unsecured revolving loan. Unsecured means should something happen to the company then creditors with more secure positions are further up 'the food chain' should the company enter into receivership. Hence the level of the overdraft given tends to be within the context of the company's financial wealth and the relationship with the bank. A number of banks offer small credit lines especially to SMEs as the first step in establishing credit. The bank views how well the business manages its cash flow. An annual credit assessment fee is often charged, naturally deducted from the account, on the anniversary of the original agreement.

Most banks offer 'corporate lending' facilities through the in-house 'Credit Committee'. The committee constitutes bankers with 'Credit Initials', often called 'Sanctioners'. A Credit Initial is related to the person making the credit approval and reflects the level of credit that person can approve. The larger the amount required, the greater is the due diligence needed to approve the loan. The size of the loan, given the risk the bank sees, may need to be well be collateralised.

The whole process is referred to as commercial lending and many of the larger loans are customised for the business borrower to provide the security and payment schedules the bank feels most comfortable with. The cost of providing a fully customised service is both expensive and time-consuming; hence the immortal banking phase: 'If you want a quick decision, it has to be no". Large commercial loans are often collateralised with a company's assets. In other words, the bank takes a secured position in the company's hierarchy of payment. The bank is amongst the first paid out in a failed situation.

Other credit techniques

Outside of commercial lending and the revolving loan area, a number of credit techniques have been created that include:

- Asset based financing;
- Loans against equity;
- Inventory financing;
- Government return financing;
- Financing via other collateral; and
- Credit default swaps.

Asset based financing

In its simplest form, a company can pledge some of its assets for a loan. These can include balance sheet items such as accounts receivable, short-term investments, inventory, equipment and assets that can be turned into cash. This can occur in three forms:

- An outright sale, such as banks selling off non-core items;
- A sale and leaseback; or
- An asset such as a precious metal being pledged for a duration of time off-site.

Sale and leaseback

Sale and leaseback often occurs in real estate when the company owns the building in which it resides. The building is acquired and a lease is drawn up for the company to continue in the premises. These transactions take time, three to six months on average, but once completed, cash is released from the premises and the monthly lease cost of the floor space becomes the ongoing cost of doing business.

Leasing other assets

Leases can be written for most things, with equipment being the most common. The lease itself can contain many clauses.

The size of the lease is determined by the value at the equipment at the start of the process and its retained value after three years.

When money is raised on a particular asset, the institute releasing the money usually holds that asset. For example, the asset can be leased. Leasing can cover any asset that has a value and the leasing agreement can last over three years. For example, most computer equipment is set over three years, with the residue value after the third year set at zero.

The person providing the money is called the Lessor and the person with the now leased asset the Lessee. The Lessor agrees to lease to the Lessee and the Lessee thereby agrees to take on lease from the Lessor the asset (equipment) on the terms and conditions of the Master Lease and any additional terms set out in the Equipment Schedule.

The agreement is in the form of a Master Lease complete with an Equipment Schedule. The Master Lease remains effective as long as any Equipment Schedule is in effect. The term of each lease is set in months or years. Extension of the Initial Term can be agreed as long as the proposed period is at least three months prior to its initial expiration date.

Before extending any equipment lease, renegotiate the price of the term, as the Lessor has had the money for the equipment and any going forward is often a bonus. That is, older the lease, the higher the chances for the Lessor making close to 100% margin.

The Lessee pays the monthly lease payments usually by direct debit in the UK and acknowledges that such lease payments are made without notice or invoice. The Lessor will make reasonable efforts to supply invoices to the Lessee but lack thereof does not alleviate the Lessee's obligation to pay.

Leases are normally calculated on a 30-day basis. Any lease payments or other sums payable not paid on the due date can be subject to a late charge. These charges can be 2% per month.

Lease payments may be varied at the sole discretion of the Lessor. For example, a common clause states that at any time, if the reference rate has altered by 0.5%, the lease payment would be pro-rated by any such change. if applied. So read the lease document carefully.

Many companies offer leasing. The actual manufacturer often provides the funding: for example, General Motors and General Electric have extensive leasing operations.

Refinancing existing assets, provided they have a value, is one way to add liquidity in the form of a lump sum, which is based on equipment leased over three years. The cost of leasing today is from 8–15% based on the availability of funds and the creditworthiness of the Lessor.

Non-payment of the lease results in the equipment being taken back by the leasing company and sold. The leasing company would then pursue any shortfall between the money due and the money being made through the sale of the asset. The chances are very high that there will be a difference, and usually a large one. It is at this point that any guarantees taken out during the leasing process are enforced.

Loans against equity

Banks follow the liquidity of equity before making a loan using the share as collateral. Banks can extend credit on shares, but usually with large margins taken against the collateral - 50% is not unusual. The bank wants the shares to cover the credit position and will often write into the contract that they have the right to sell should the equity value look endangered. This usually means the top 100 shares have collateral that meets the bank's criteria, albeit with healthy safety margins. Other equity positions are at the bank's discretion. Directors of a company whose shares have been placed have to notify the authorities.

Inventory financing

Inventory financing can be used by manufacturers making products, e.g. cars where inventory tends to form a significant percentage of assets. A loan can be made to a manufacturer using its inventory as collateral.

Where companies deal in products which have a market value, e.g. wine, then banks can to grant credit against the inventory. The credit amount is often at a sharp discount to the wholesale price, with the bank becoming the owner of the goods should something happen to the company

Financing via other collateral

Contracts signed with creditworthy parties can be used as collateral provided the length of contract exceeds three years. Often a group of contracts can be put together and pledged against the extension of credit. Margins are high, and provided the bank is comfortable with the credit risk, credit is extended. Collateralisation is used extensively in the money market to guarantee bonds. This methodology has created bonds backed by everything from credit card receivables, through David Bowie's music royalties, to mortgage-backed guarantees and, of course, sub-prime bonds.

Approvals in the UK

A Warwick University report noted that, in contrast to bank loans, rejection rates for leasing and hire purchase agreements appear to have been largely unaffected by the credit crisis: 2.7% of applicants in 2008 were turned down compared with 3% in 2001-4. However, analysis of the distribution of bank loan rejections in 2005-8 shows that 73.5% of all overdraft rejections in that period took place in 2007-2008. Also 81.2% of all term loan rejections in the period 2005-8 took place in 2007-2008. If 2007-2008 had been an unexceptional year, only one-third of all rejections in 2005-8 would have been expected in 2007-2008.

Looking at reasons for rejection, overdraft rejections due to the firm having no security/collateral have more than doubled in 2005-2008 (accounting for 9.5% of overdraft rejections; up from 4.1% in 2001-4); and rejections due to the firm's industry being too risky have almost doubled in 2005-8 (from 2.4%, in 2001-4, to 4.6% in 2005- 08).

Collateral and security has become important to gain access to credit. The assets put up for collateral need to be readily converted into cash. The security will also be assessed and often guarantees will be requested.

Personal Guarantees (PGs)

A personal guarantee is a promise by a person or an entity to assume a debt obligation in the event of non-payment by the borrower. The loan agreement should make it clear exactly what security the bank needs. Guarantees can be provided by:

- You, especially if you run a limited company;
- Other people involved in the business, usually equity holders;
- A benefactor or patron.

Banks may also ask another person or business to act as a guarantor, for example the customer. The reason is simple: the banks want a source of credit that, if the interest repayments and capital are not met in part or whole, then the guarantor pays that part or all of the loan and interest that is missing.

In a limited company, banks and major creditors will usually require personal guarantees from the company directors or major shareholders. Limited liability protects shareholders from being sued by the business' creditors for their personal assets. Where a personal guarantee for a bank loan is issued, the guarantor can be held personally liable for the debt. This means the guarantor can be sued for the repayment and personal assets ceased.

Wherever possible, ensure that personal guarantees only apply to specific debts or loans. An unspecified guarantee could render the guarantor liable for all of the losses of the business up to the amount of the guarantee. Under the UK lending code, guarantees given in support of bank account borrowing must not be for an unlimited amount.

PGs are often used in amounts over £20,000 and especially when collateral is being pledged against the credit or lease being undertaken. The guarantor acts as lender of last resort and as such needs to be clear exactly what they are guaranteeing should the worst situation occur.

Provision of credit – case study

An SME domestic furniture retailer operating in Ireland requires the provision of up to €10-15 million credit in order to provide its retail customers with consumer finance; this is necessary to compete with its major competitor, whose chief advantage is its ability to offer credit terms to their customers, which drives the rationale for consumer credit in Ireland. The Irish banks have effectively withdrawn from this market sector.

The business case is presented below.

Summary

Retailer Ltd is a UK-registered limited company incorporated in and operating stores throughout the Republic of Ireland. Retailer sells budget sofas, beds and other furniture from large retail park units. The intensively-marketed, low-cost business model has proved highly successful, especially in the present climate.

Retailer now seeks to offer instalment and buy-now-pay-later facilities to reach a wider customer base and continue its rapid expansion. It is intended that this customer offering be funded by a combination of trade profits and bank debt.

Strategy

1. *Designer living rooms at discount prices in a fun atmosphere*
    - The store design, marketing and staff training all focus on a consistently friendly and approachable retail experience.
2. *Cost control has been central to the achievements to date*
    - Low structural overheads mirror the Wal-Mart business model.

3. *Store costs are lower than competitors*
    - Sources units in the best locations, often on short leases, allowing substantial savings against comparable rates.
4. *Shop fits are undertaken quickly and economically*
    - In line with the Wal-Mart model, Retailer can fit out a store from shell to opening in 3-4 weeks including 85 -100 partitioned, lighted rooms.
5. *Efficient delivery*
    - One central warehouse in Dublin, which delivers to each store.
6. *Super-fast delivery*
    - The leading 20% of product lines representing 80% of sales are delivered the next day. This compares very favourably to the more typical 16-week lead time offered by many competitors.
7. *Room packages*
    - The stores display coordinated furniture products in attractive room settings, with discounts for whole room packages: a one-stop model, which is well established in the USA.
8. *Convenient store hours*
    - Trading hours are between 10 am and 6pm, seven days a week, with late night opening on Thursdays.
9. *Memorable service levels*
    - Retailer literally has a 'red carpet delivery service'. A red carpet is rolled out over the customer's doorway to ensure no mud is taken into the house, the sofa is fully unwrapped and legs attached. A thank-you note is placed on the new sofa together with a gift of chocolates. Service levels are monitored centrally and stores are incentivised to score highly.

Target market

The target demographic is mass-market lower to middle income brackets, with purchasers tending to be buying for their first property or redecorating when offspring have left the home. Average spend is £1,300 and sales are often driven by extensively-marketed promotions which often include free televisions or ancillary furniture.

Management team

The four Board members have extensive retail expertise and are supported by 48 directly employed staff in sales (18), distribution (21) and administration (9). Ongoing and intensive training is central to the strong service delivery.

Merchandise

Sofas are directly sourced from China, the beds in the UK and, to a lesser extent, Vietnam. No middlemen are involved and delivery times from the Far East to UK are 8–18 weeks. The buyer visits the manufacturers monthly and the product is therefore able to be updated and tweaked far more quickly than competitors. The lines are innovative, varied and able to respond to changes in fashion very quickly.

Competitive analysis

Retailer competes against DFS, Reid's and Harvey Norman and the table below shows the strength and weakness of each against what the customer thinks is important.

	Retailer		DFS		Reids'		Harvey Norman		Customer Importance
FACTOR	**Strength**	**Weakness**	**Strength**	**Weakness**	**Strength**	**Weakness**	**Strength**	**Weakness**	**Scale: 5 top 1 least**
Products	X		X					X	5
Price	X			X		X			5
Quality	X		X						4
Selection	X		X			X	X		3
Service	X		X						3
Delivery speed	X			X					3
Stability	X		X						3
Expertise	X		X			X			3
Credit policies			X		X		X		3
Advertising	X		X						3

Financials

The P&L from 2007 to 2011 actual plus a forecast for 2012 are shown below:

Retailer Ltd
Profit and Loss Account

	Actual			Forecast
Figures in €	**2007**	**2009**	**2011**	**2012**
Turnover	4,061,000	8,359,000	13,900,000	17,000,000
Cost of sales	1,960,000	3,959,000	7,645,000	9,350,000
Gross profit	2,101,000	4,400,000	6,255,000	7,650,000
Administration	1,891,000	4,149,000	6,029,000	7,150,000
Profit before tax	210,000	251,000	226,000	500,000

Financial projections

The table below shows the impact of consumer credit on the business, with the business assumptions made against the various line elements. The key assumptions for the loan are:

- Cost of money to Retailer Ltd is 7%
- Cost of credit to customer is 23%
- Write-off of credit to customer is 1%
- Administration fee to customer is 3%
- Credit score fee is €0.6

Projections

All figures in €	Assumptions	Year 1	Year 2	Year 3
Projected furniture sales	1.2	39,215,686	47,058,824	56,470,588
Projected % of sales on credit		30%	30%	30%
Gross credit business		11,764,706	14,117,647	16,941,176
Accept rate	85%	85%	85%	85%
Potential credit sales		10,000,000	12,000,000	14,400,000
Average size of order	1,500	1,500	1,500	1,500
Deposit levels	40%	4,000,000	4,800,000	5,760,000
Customer charges				
Administration fees	3%	180,000	216,000	259,200
Insurance income (4% of potential credit sales, 50% customer cover for the insurance)	2.0%	200,000	240,000	288,000
Retail reimbursement	60%	6,000,000	7,200,000	8,640,000
Written credit sales		6,380,000	7,656,000	9,187,200
Average size of credit	945	945	945	945
Average contract length in months		48	48	48
Income		**Year 1**	**Year 2**	**Year 3**
Interest earned	22.99%	776,328	2,208,468	3,418,575
Interest costs	7.0%	(184,665)	(555,511)	(824,970)
Total income		971,663	2,108,957	3,140,805
Expenses		**Year 1**	**Year 2**	**Year 3**
Account inquire cost	€ 2.20	14,667	17,600	21,120
Scorecard cost	€ 0.60	4,051	4,861	5,833
Legal fees		50,000	0	0
IT costs		14,400	14,400	14,400
Staff admin	4%	255,200	306,240	367,488
Other admin costs	2%	127,600	153,120	183,744
Promotional costs	1%	60,000	72,000	86,400
Debt collection cost	3%	143,550	229,680	275,616
Bad debts	1%	47,850	76,560	91,872
Depreciation	48	8,250	14,500	14,500
Cost of insurance (50% of insurance income)	50%	100,000	120,000	144,000
Total overheads		825,567	1,008,961	1,051,853
Net profit		146,096	1,099,996	2,088,952
Cumulative profit		146,096	1,246,092	3,882,243

Cash flow		Year 1	Year 2	Year 3
PBT		146,096	1,099,996	2,088,952
Depreciation		8,250	14,500	14,500
Provision for bad debt		47,850	76,560	76,560
Changes in working capital		(651,485)	(667,389)	(626,905)
Finance debtors		5,918,703	11,841,091	17,251,652
Total WC		5,918,703	11,841,091	17,251,652
Funds from operations		(449,289)	523,667	1,553,107
Capital expenditure		33,000	25,000	25,000
Plant and machinery		15,000	15,000	15,000
IT costs		18,000	10,000	10,000
Free cash flow		(482,289)	498,667	1,528,107

Collateral to liquidity

The balance sheet shows assets of €2.7 million valued at the traditional method. Looking at the assets on a 30-day liquidation basis shows the discount to realise the cash is 60%. Even here the largest component, the inventory, could well be over valued at 50% of the finished goods value. The easiest to value is cash at 100% and the motor vehicles at 75% of book value. Plant/machinery and fixture/fittings often have little value, so 10% as a converter to cash is fair.

	Balance sheet value	Risk factor	Liquid value
Fixed assets			
Plant/Machinery	50,000	10%	5,000
Fixture/Fittings	640,000	10%	64,000
Motors	40,000	75%	30,000
Current assets			
Stock	2,000,000	50%	1,000,000
Cash	23,000	100%	23,000
Total	2,753,000	Average: 41%	1,122,000

As the company is limited, the shareholders fund of €1.5 million has little liquidity value.

Obligations

Bank loans less than 12 months of €535,000 and over 12 months of €120,000 for a total of €655,000. These are guaranteed by a fixed and floating charge on the assets of the company, personal guarantees and a property lien on one of the director's property.

Security for the lender

The provider of the funds would have the first lien over the 'credit book'. The credit book can be structured in a way that it can be floated off and sold into the market. This is the traditional US model for home mortgages. The provider of credit for the home has the mortgage put into a pack and sold off. It was this approach, coupled with little due diligence and poor credit scoring, that led to the sub-prime lending crisis.

Status

The market is reluctant to fund this initiative. The Irish banks have virtually no appetite for this type of funding. The London market is concerned over money going into the Irish economy. The financials show a healthy return, yet the markets lack confidence. People are buying sofas and will continue to do so in increasing numbers as the economy expands. The competitor DFS has the credit available and will continue to offer this option.

The future

The banks' appetite for credit is defined by capital equity, which from 2019 will be a 6.7 multiple of that capital. This is about 25% less than it is today. Consequently, credit is becoming a scarce resource. As such, the price and levels of credit approval will rise. In addition, more decisions will be made centrally, with information collected from a number of sources, including credit bureaux.

SMEs need cash to grow. The faster the business grows, the greater the need for cash. Banks will continue to be a source of funding. However, actually receiving credit on today's banking behaviour means the requester for credit needs to be almost perfect; this requires that the credit score has to match the bank's profile of what is required. It is credit scoring which will determine the approval of credit. If the SME does not meet that score, then the chances of overturning the fail will be very difficult and alternative sources of credit need to be sourced. The use of asset finance techniques to facilitate the need for cash will accelerate.

The credit report will be central to any assessment by a bank or non-bank. SME Boards and directors will therefore need to be advised of its status and take steps to make it acceptable to the banks. The better the credit report, the more the chances of the computer screening accepting and approving the credit are increased.

The future of credit approval for SMEs will be down to mathematical formulae. It will cost too much for banks to do anything else. Only when the potential financial numbers look big or there are circumstances that are unique will banks assign people to make a judgement.

In the future, governments will take a greater role in assisting SMEs in obtaining credit, as in most countries, SMEs account for at least 50% of the economy. To help underpin the credit being issued by the banks to SMEs, the government may take some of the risk out of this sector, having agreed to take a set percentage, e.g. 25%, of the write-off should the SME fail.

CHAPTER 8
THE INVESTMENT PYRAMID VERSUS THE CREDIT LADDER

Questions for SME directors

- What is your net interest income between the interest generated by the cash and the cost of the credit being used?
- When comparing your company's investment pyramid to the credit ladder, what makes you feel comfortable and/or uncomfortable?

Key considerations

- Managing the Net Interest Income;
- Comparing investment against credit.

Net Interest Income (NII)

The difference between the revenues generated from interest on the loan and the cost of the money to provide that loan is called the Net Interest Income. For banks this is a key measurement because it indicates the interest spreads between its loans and its deposits. Banks have a wide range of loan rates based on time span and risk profile. To support the loan business banks use their clients' deposits, deposits from other financial institutions, and the money markets. The use of the money markets was rampant especially in the early part of this century, but since the credit market correction in 2007 due to sub-prime loans, access to the money market is difficult. Extensive regulations have also been enacted to help prevent a repeat of the credit crisis.

To gain a wide NII, the bank seeks to pay the lowest amount allowable for its deposits and charge the highest amount possible for its loans. In the US, many of the smaller banks have a policy of a minimum of 5% spread on top of the base bank rate for new loans. Historically, loans to companies with good credit ratings were often made at 1–2% above base. Blue chip companies often have a better credit rating than their banks and could command interest rates at less than 1% over base.

Similarly in cash management, the company receives interest on deposits and is charged interest on any loans or overdrafts. The difference between the two is often dramatic and not in the favour of the company. Money held in the bank account should be put to work. The banks are often tempered by their positions on the deposit side as compared to its loans. If, for example, the bank is deposit-rich, the need to pay interest on its deposit base is reduced, resulting in rates slightly above 0% for immediate access to the cash.

When banks need deposits (and this is currently a major priority for many banks, especially in the US and Europe), then the chances of offering better interest rates are more common. Deposits for banks come with the added criteria that they have to be stable and that the money should not leave as quickly as it arrives. Often termed 'hot money', this type of cash needs incentives to stay.

Comparing the pyramid with the ladder

Comparison of the investment pyramid against the credit ladder is an indicator of how the cash situation is poised. Having a great investment pyramid with few credit facilities suggests a cash-rich company. An investment pyramid in which the credit ladder is on balance suggests an ongoing working company. At the point where the credit ladder starts to exceed the investment pyramid, then cash flow issues are likely. The more these issues persist, the greater the need for cash and the greater the chance of the credit facility becoming expensive. As this expense grows, the ladder starts to pull the pyramid towards a negative situation.

Figure 8.1: The investment pyramid vs the credit ladder (1)

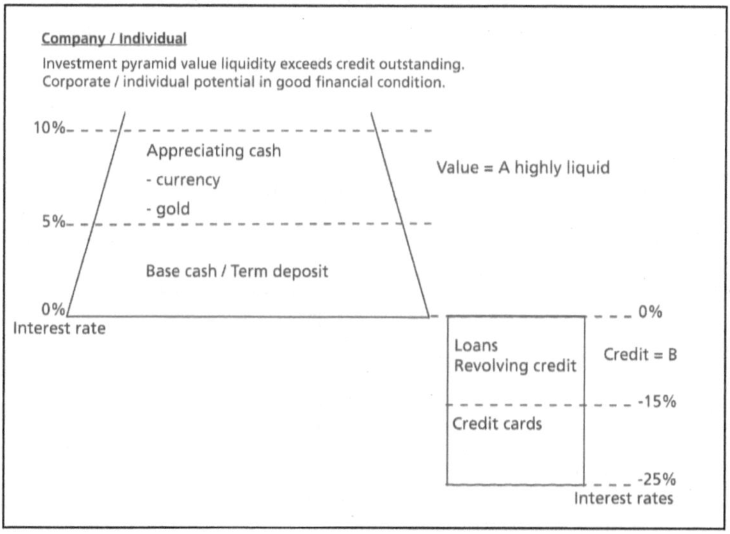

Company / Individual

Investment pyramid value liquidity exceeds credit outstanding.
Corporate / individual potential in good financial condition.

10%
Appreciating cash
- currency
- gold
Value = A highly liquid
5%
Base cash / Term deposit
0%
Interest rate

0%
Loans
Revolving credit
Credit = B
-15%
Credit cards
-25%
Interest rates

Source: Author

Figure 8.2: The investment pyramid vs the credit ladder (2)

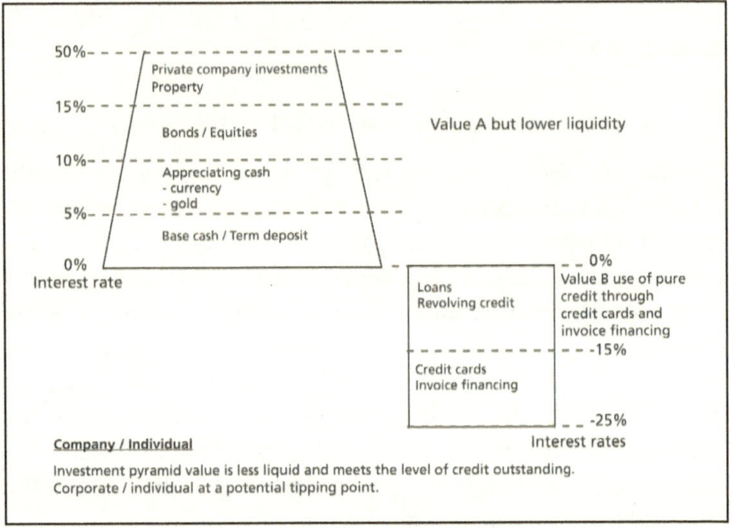

Source: Author

Figure 8.3: The investment pyramid vs the credit ladder (3)

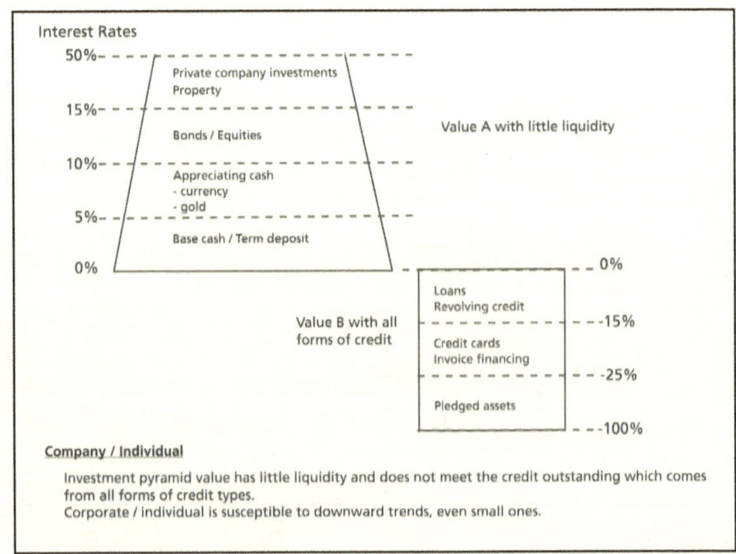

Source: Author

Leveraging and deleveraging

The comparison shows where the money is and where it is going. When the cash flow allows, the paying back of debt should start with the highest interest rate being charged. The faster those debts are retired, the more money there is to pay off the next level of debt. The process feeds on itself and the debt picture becomes easier to handle and moves to a manageable level. This is called leverage, and leverage comes at a price which needs to be covered each month. Banks with the new proposed Basel III of 15% will have a 7 to 1 leverage.

For an indication of the level of liquidity of the SME is at a given time, try the following test and then compare Sum A against Sum B. The comparison is a guide to liquidity; if the credit ladder exceeds the investment pyramid, then liquidity is probably a concern.

Table 8.1: Comparing the investment pyramid with the credit ladder

Investment pyramid	Amount	Score
Step 1	Cash	Amount x 5
Step 2	Term deposits	Amount x 4
Step 3	Cash alternatives	Amount x 3
Step 4	Bonds, equities and properties	Amount x 2
Step 5	Private companies, art, collectables	Amount x 1
Total Score		SUM A

Credit ladder	Amount	Score
Step 1	0 to 10%	Amount x 1
Step 2	10% to 20%	Amount x 2
Step 3	20% to 30%	Amount x 3
Step 4	30% to 50%	Amount x 4
Step 5	Over 50%	Amount x 5
Total Score		SUM B

Deleveraging is occurring across households in many countries. 'Working out of Debt', a McKinsey report in January 2012 showed that US household debt outstanding fell by $584 billion (4%) from the end of 2008 through the second quarter of 2011. Defaults account for about 70% and 80% of the decrease in mortgage debt and consumer credit, respectively. It is estimated that up to 35% of the defaults resulted from strategic decisions by households to walk away from their homes, since they owed far more than their properties were worth. This option is available in the US; it is not necessarily an option in other countries. As of the second quarter of 2011, the ratio of household debt to income had fallen by 11% from the start of the financial crisis.

During the 1990s, Sweden and Finland had similar banking crises, recessions, and deleveraging. In both, the ratio of household debt to income declined by roughly 30% from its peak.

Three years on from the start of the financial crisis, UK households have deleveraged, with the ratio of debt to disposable income falling from 156% in the fourth quarter of 2008 to 146% in second quarter of 2011. Residential mortgages have grown slowly, offsetting some of the £25 billion decline in consumer credit.

Similarly in Spain, household debt to disposable income has fallen by 4%. Spanish corporations hold twice as much debt relative to national output as US companies, and six times as much as German companies.

The future

Getting the balance between investment and credit right is an age-old issue. The days of easy and cheap credit appear numbered. To get credit, a credit report is needed and to get a good rating it has to show credits being taken and repaid. So credit is a part of the financial make-up.

Investments need to be biased towards liquidity. The spectacular gains are just that – something that happens a few times in a decade. The need for liquidity is to provide flexibility to take opportunities as they arise.

The least risky positioning is towards the bottom of the pyramid and towards the top of the ladder.

For banks, this positioning is part of their governance and monitored by the assets and liabilities committee. Rarely do assets and liabilities balance exactly. Each bank will have its own view on the mix, although it is now biased towards greater liquidity.

SMEs will need to focus more on their collection of assets and liabilities and putting them to greater use. Going forward, collateralisation of credit is on the rise and an exit or liquidity route is required. Banks have the right to call in credit, usually at any time, and did so often during the crisis, regardless of the business payment history. Liquidity is therefore the key at such events.

As the majority of credit assessment will be through credit scoring, the need to have an acceptable credit rating is paramount. Banks are moving into the centralisation of credit and are using algorithms to manage the portfolio to an agreed level of risk. Those banks that have taken governments bailouts will ensure that they are prudent. This prudence will leave the level of credit approval for unsecured activities almost unattainable, or if attainable, at a high price. Consequently, SMEs need to manage their credit reports and have collateral that can be monetised quickly.

CHAPTER 9
PAYMENTS

Questions for SME directors

- What percentage of our payments are received and paid by direct debit?
- If have we been paying by direct debit for a while, are all the direct debits still valid, as 10% are often for services not required, e.g. telephones?
- Is our bank account reconciled automatically and daily?
- What is our payments volume and do we qualify for a discount?

Key considerations

- Use of immediate payments over being paid by common forms of payment, both bank and non-bank;
- Management of payment timelines standards;
- If in two or more European countries, use Single European Payment Area (SEPA);
- Management of payment fees.

Creating harmonised payments

THE PAYMENT LANDSCAPE is changing. No more cheques in the post or checks in the mail. Immediate payment is now available through 'Faster Payments' in the UK and worldwide through warehouse accounts suppliers such as PayPal.

Each country has evolved its own payment and clearing systems. Each also has its specific rules surrounding corporate governance. The central banks historically had a lock on their own unique payment clearing rules and regulations. These rules are becoming synchronised with each other as the world is becoming more interconnected. The level of commerce over the internet, especially when buying and selling in multiple countries, is growing rapidly.

In Asia, payments cover a broad spectrum of requirements, with varying payment formats and systems. In some countries, paper instruments are more commonly accepted and in others, electronic payments are the norm. Domestic payments infrastructure is developed in some countries whilst this is still evolving in others.

With the creation of the euro, the EU set out to harmonise the money being moved between the EU countries. Studies made prior to the establishment of the euro showed that fees for international rather than local payments often cost often 10 times as much as the domestic charge. Since 2001 a directive (2560/2001) limited bank fees on cross-border transactions to a similar level to domestic charges.

Float and timeframes

In 2006, the EU published the Single Euro Payment Area (SEPA) scheme book which outlawed float. It is in the banking community's self-interest to keep money in the system, unallocated to any account for as long as possible. This is called float. Float is the money earned by banks on money in transit between accounts. Banks invest this 'free' money into interest or fee earning instruments (investment vehicles) and retain the money they generate. As the money is free, i.e. the bank does not have to pay interest on the money, the bank's margin on float is 100%.

Float has to be balanced between customer service and any associated laws, based on the timeframe. The EU defines this timeframe as five working days for the eurozone. After that timeframe, claims for compensation against the originating bank are permitted. Otherwise, the time between an account being credited after one that has been debited can become unacceptably long. Before the EU regulation, a cross-border payment could take as long as a month. The length of time a bank can keep funds in transit often becomes a political issue in many countries.

In the UK, for example, the banks use BACS, an Automated Clearing House (ACH), which moves money after three business days. This timeframe was taken as a standard because it matched the same amount of time it would take a cheque to clear, prior to automation. Technically, payments can be done instantaneously; the UK now offers instant payments termed 'Faster Payments' through the bank-owned VocaLink company,

Faster Payments can be used to move money in less than 15 minutes, provided the bank sending the money and the bank receiving it have installed the required software and procedures into their IT environment. If they have not, the payments follow the BACS route. Faster payments can go up to any amount and from 1 January 2012, most banks will send up to £100,000. The European Payment Services Directive also became law on the same day and euro payments must be completed in D+1. That is, payments need to be paid by the bank within two working days anywhere in the euro zone.

Same/next day funds transfers – urgent payments

Increasing global complexities and industry competitiveness demand maximum convenience, flexibility and cost-effectiveness in managing internal payments.

When a business needs to disburse funds for immediate delivery or needs to accommodate suppliers who want funds credited directly to their accounts, the capability to provide the credit for payment to the beneficiary bank account for same-day payment regardless of currency depends upon:

- Meeting applicable cut-off times;
- The ability of beneficiary bank to receive electronic funds transfers;
- Intervening holidays and non-business days in country of currency;
- Funds transfer instructions requiring a repair may be delayed;
- Complete counterpart account and bank details.

Other payment methods

Cheques

The use of a cheque for payment peaked in the UK in 1990 with 11 million cheques issued. In 2010, 3.1 million cheques were issued and throughout 2011 a decline of 12% was evident. In many countries, for example Scandinavia, cheques virtually do not exist. The USA is the world's biggest user of cheques, but in the 10 years from 2001 to 2010, cheques have gone from being the dominant form of payment to 22% of all payments. The cheque trend is one of continued global decline. Globally, in 2005 22% of non-cash payments were made by cheque and by 2009 the figure had dropped to 16%.

The UK operates on a '2-4-6' time system for cheque clearing. That is, the cheque is presented to the bank on day 0; after day 2 the bank would pay interest, if applicable. On day 4 the bank can allow money to be withdrawn and by day 6 the money has been cleared and settled.

Figure 9.1: Cheque (paper) payment flow

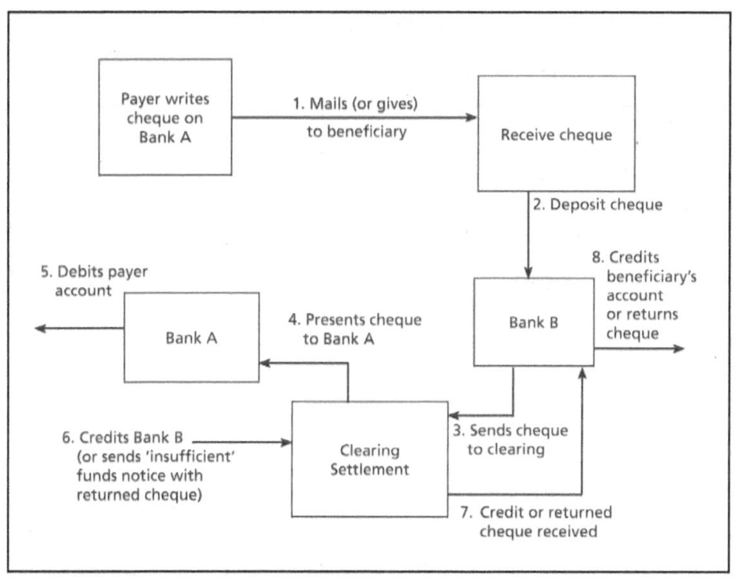

Source: Author

Automated Clearing House (ACH) payments

As cheques have declined in use, electronic payments have increased. In the UK in 2011, 59% of all payments processed by BACS were direct debits (DD), 39% were direct credits, and 2% standing orders. The average value of a DD was £313 in Q3 2011. Over 80% of adults in the UK have at least one DD and they are used by over 100,000 business and organisations.

In the US, the ACH network is a batch processing, store and forward system, governed by the NACHA Operating Rule Book. (NACHA is the US Electronic Payment Association). The ACH connects financial institutions which batch the transactions as they are received and then forward them at predetermined periods into the network. The number of transactions in the first half of 2011 exceeded 8 billion and grew 2.7% in the 2nd quarter as compared to the previous year. The average transaction amount is $2,100. The schedule of fees for 2012 for a Depositary Financial Institution, e.g. a bank, is $0.000145 per item plus an annual fee of $144.

Figure 9.2: ACH payment

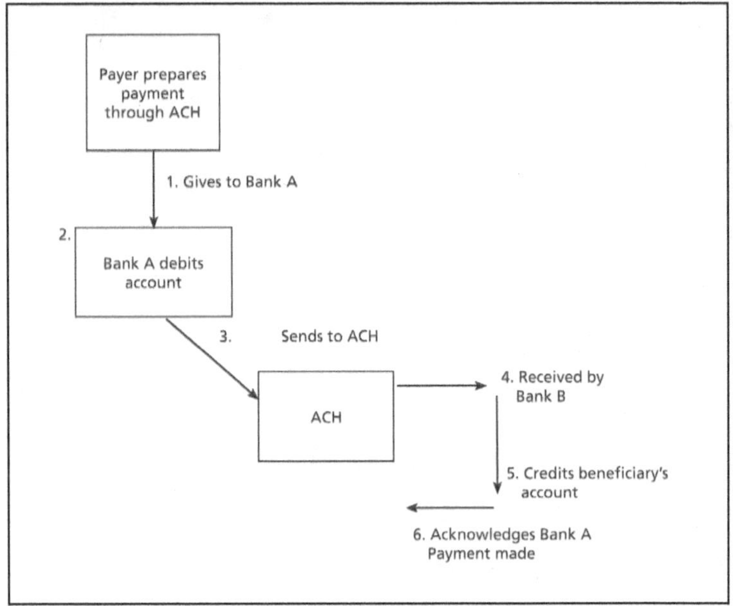

Source: Author

ACH for non-urgent payments

Electronic payments are processed through local country clearing systems rather than through the traditional funds transfers that clear through regional clearings systems such as CHIPS or EBA. ACH payments are traditionally low-value, non-urgent payments processed with value dates of two to five days depending on the clearing country. For example, the EU is setting the standard across its member countries of three working days for SEPA (Single European Payment Area). The actual size of the payment is irrelevant provided it is non-urgent.

The standard requirement for processing ACH payments is maintenance of a clearing account in each country where the company makes payments. The benefits include:

- No administration or cost of having international bank accounts to process local electronic payments;
- A single point of entry to process multiple payment types to multiple countries in multiple currencies;
- Full audit trails and management reports.

Direct debit

A direct debit is an extension of a single ACH payment. A DD is an instrument originated by a customer authorising the bank to pay a beneficiary by collecting monies from the customer's account. A DD allows for the amount collected to be processed provided the customer has been informed in advance. Should a DD bounce (note the cheque process reference), then as long as the customer is informed, the DD can be reinstated and the money taken provided there are funds in the account.

In the US, this type of payment is often referred to as pull service. That is, the money is taken out of the account (pulled) on agreed terms.

Figure 9.3: Direct debit payment

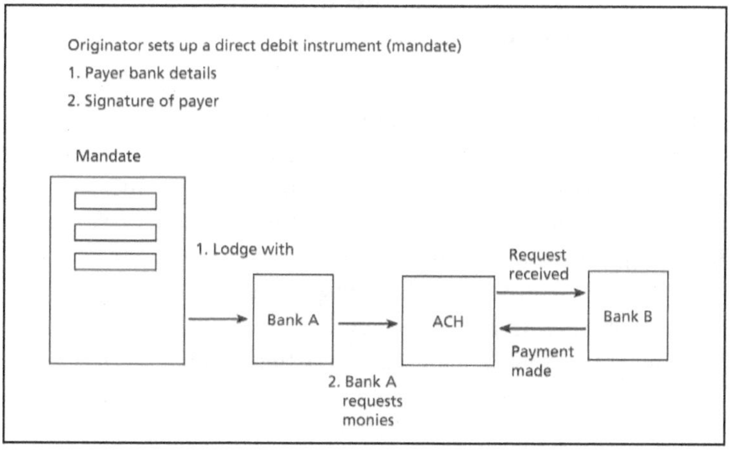

Originator sets up a direct debit instrument (mandate)
1. Payer bank details
2. Signature of payer
Mandate
1. Lodge with
Bank A
ACH
Request received
Bank B
Payment made
2. Bank A requests monies

Source: Author

SEPA Direct Debit (SDD)

The SEPA Core Direct Debit Scheme – like any other direct debit scheme – is based on the following concept: "I request money from someone else, with their preapproval, and credit it to myself".

The SEPA mandate is an authorisation from a debtor (a customer purchasing goods or services) to the creditor (a retailer or service provider) to collect payments automatically from their bank account. This is called SEPA Direct Debit and has the following characteristics:

- Mandate forms to be completed by customers are usually provided by creditors themselves;
- The EPC now offers guidance to creditors on the creation of streamlined, easy-to-use SEPA mandates;
- In addition, the EPC provides translations of the mandate text as specified in the SEPA Core Direct Debit Scheme Rulebook into the SEPA languages;
- 16 to 18 million businesses in the euro area and all public administrations collecting payments in SEPA are now in a position to create the user-friendly SEPA mandate forms which best meets their needs.

The SEPA Core Direct Debit (SDD) Scheme Rulebook defines the rules for the content of SEPA mandates (section 4.7.2 – The Mandate). Customers who complete and sign such forms will eventually provide virtually the same information on a SEPA mandate as in any mandate issued under most legacy direct debit schemes today.

The EBA (European Banking Association) reported a volume of 6.5 million transactions per day in the 4th quarter 2011, which is double the volume for the 1st quarter 2011.

Table 9.1: Payment systems comparison

Payment method performance	Time
Domestic	
Cheque Automatic Clearing House	Minimum 5 days
One-off payment	24 hours
Direct Debit	3 days
Faster Payments (UK)	15 minutes
International	
Bank-to-bank	24 hours
SWIFT – transporter, not payment	15 minutes
PayPal	same day
Cheque (UK)	minimum 10 days
Check (US) – 21 Act allows a physical check to be replaced by a digital one	Dependent on bank – some allow credit same day and reverse out if money is not forthcoming
SEPA Direct Debits (SDD)	3 days (Europe only)

Local direct debit schemes vs. SEPA

In many SEPA countries, mandates that were issued by a debtor under existing national direct debit schemes do not conform to the SEPA Mandate. To facilitate the changeover to the SEPA Direct Debit Scheme, however, it is imperative that the millions of mandates in place today can indeed be used under the SEPA Scheme, at least for a transition period. EU Member States must, where necessary, create legislative solutions to ensure the continued legal validity of existing mandates under the SEPA Direct Debit Scheme. The principles are:

- The SEPA Direct Debit aims to make every DD scheme in Europe identical so payments can flow through the eurozone efficiently. It is based on the same principle as the local DD programs which permit the request of money from someone else with their prior approval and a credit to the requestor.

- The payer and the biller must each hold an account with a payment service provider (PSP) located within SEPA.
- The account maybe in euros or any other SEPA currency; however, the transfer between the payer's bank and the biller's bank always takes place in euros.
- SDD allows a biller to collect from a payer's account provided a signed Mandate has been given to the payer by the biller. The Mandate is different from the local DD and legally, often an existing Mandate can not be novated (depends on the law in each country) into a SDD without a new Mandate being signed.
- The new Mandates require additional information, including IBAN (International Bank Account Number) and BIC (Bank Identifier Code – often called the SWIFT number).

It is estimated that up to 10% of the existing Mandates are for services and products are now not currently required by the payer. Any new Mandate will probably provoke the need to examine the need to continue the service. The payer will look anew at what have been paid previously and may request a refund. Hence the holders of legacy mandates want the move to SDD from DD to be as seamless as possible, and if available simply novate the DD into SDD. Each country has different novation laws so the legacy mandates will either be completed without a new signed agreement, or a new agreement must be signed. All new DD mandates are converted to SDD mandates once SEPA becomes legally binding. The standardised messages can include up to seven reasons for a rejection. On 15 February 2012, the European Parliament agreed the SEPA end-date, making it legally binding for banks to offer SEPA payment processes from 1 February 2014.

E-payments

The term e-payments is often used to describe the online payment services offered by banks. It is an electronic platform that can process a variety of payments over the internet. The platforms are designed to be secure and available for credit and debit cards. Benefits are real-time authorisation and fast payment. A merchant acquirer account number is needed when selling goods and services requiring card payment. Specialist companies look after merchant payments through credit and debit cards, as the merchants themselves are constantly monitored for credit, ethical and moral reasons.

M-payments

Mobile payments are tipped to be the fastest growing area. Research company Juniper noted in June 2011 that mobile payments users are set to grow by 40%, to reach 2.5 billion globally. Research undertaken by an independent company ACCORD, around the same time held 10,000 interviews which suggests the following for mobile payments:

- Strong appeal from 42% in the UK to 56% in Malaysia;
- SME appeal in each country was 70%;
- SMEs liked the ability to be paid straight away;
- Security is required alongside the convenience;
- Willingness to incur a fee for immediate payment especially in Canada (49%), Germany (47%) and the USA (47%).

Steve Jobs once commented that he rarely used focus groups as people could not see or grasp a new product until it was there. Mobile payments probably falls into this category.

In the UK, Barclays is offering Pingit, an instant account-to-account application for a smartphone user. Within 48 hours of the launch in February 2012, over 20,000 applications were downloaded. Barclays is not charging for the service and has completed the technology to interface smartphones with its core systems. Barclays expects to make its money through cross-selling products and adding new clients.

A number of countries have established industry bodies to take the lead in developing a non- priority platform. These include Japan, South Korea and France. In the UK, the UK Payments Council has appointed VocaLink to provide a central database that allows bank customers to link their mobile numbers to their account for mobile payments. The reason for this move is to create a common infrastructure for all banks and non-banks.

Warehouse accounts

Warehouse accounts held by non-banks offer an alternative payment process to the banking structure.

Bank accounts can now be augmented by warehouse accounts offered by non-bank organisations; this is a relatively recent development. These non-banks use the banking infrastructure, so money does not actually leave the system. With accounts held by non-banks, the money coming out of a bank account or off a credit card is first lodged in the warehouse account. The holder of that account can then move money to another person with a warehouse account. The non-bank gives the warehouse account holder a 24 x 7 capability to pay and receive money from anywhere around the world.

The downside is that these accounts are not insured as bank accounts are under deposit protection schemes, and therefore should the non-bank provider fail, the money in the warehouse account would be lost. Benefits include prompt and convenient payment and no account fees, and the capability to use credit cards to fund the business.

The largest provider of this approach is PayPal with 230 million accounts worldwide, which competes with the traditional banking payment system known as correspondent banking.

See 'Payment fees' below for a comparison of bank and warehouse account charges.

Figure 9.4: Warehouse account process (1)

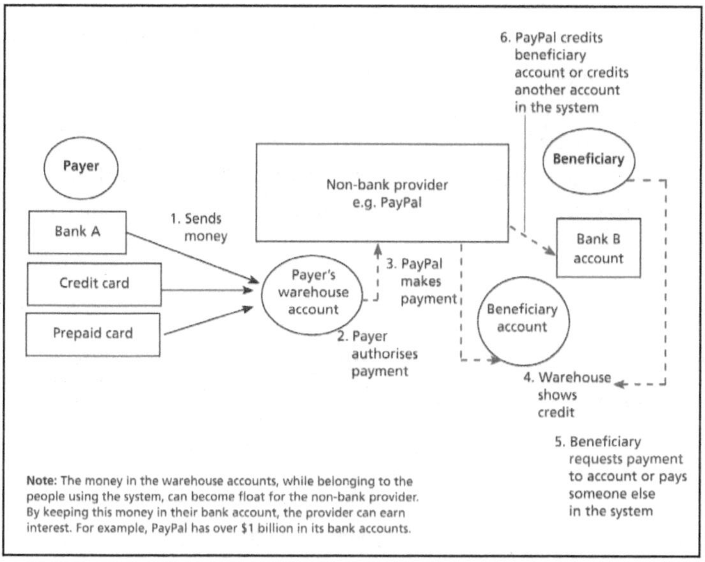

6. PayPal credits beneficiary account or credits another account in the system
Payer
Non-bank provider e.g. PayPal
Beneficiary
Bank A
1. Sends money
Bank B account
Credit card
Payer's warehouse account
3. PayPal makes payment
Prepaid card
Beneficiary account
2. Payer authorises payment
4. Warehouse shows credit
5. Beneficiary requests payment to account or pays someone else in the system
Note: The money in the warehouse accounts, while belonging to the people using the system, can become float for the non-bank provider. By keeping this money in their bank account, the provider can earn interest. For example, PayPal has over $1 billion in its bank accounts.

Source: Author

Figure 9.5: Warehouse account process (2)

Non-bank processer
Company A / individual
Warehouse account A
Sends credit to account B
Warehouse account B
Company B / individual
Country A
Credit information only – cash stays in banking infrastructure
Country B
credit
Company B can pull down credit
Existing banking infrastructure
Non-bank Bank accounts
debit
credit
Country B
Bank account for Company A
movement of money
Country A
debit
Country A

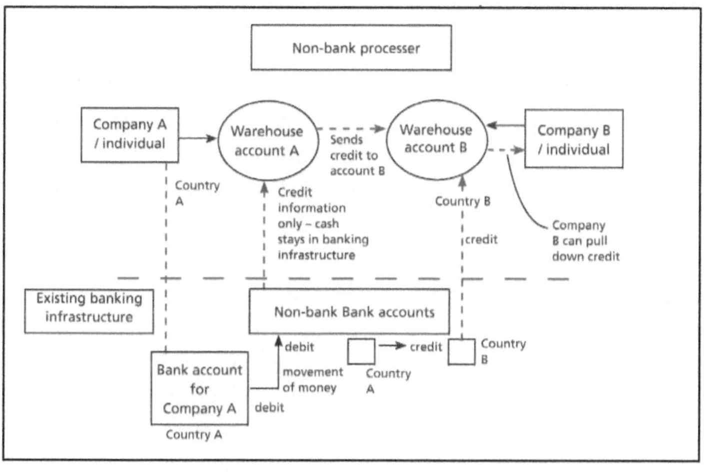

Source: Author

Value dating

This is the time when a credit to the account can actually be used. The credit may be posted to the account, and seen on the account, but the actual use of funds is only available once the 'credit' instrument has cleared. The use of value dates helps protect the bank from monies not arriving from the other bank should the transaction be returned unpaid from the other bank.

Figure 9.6: Value dating

Bank Account	Today	Day 1	Day 2	Day 3	Day 4
Balance in Account	1000	-	-	-	-
Value dated transactions (2 days)	500	500	500	-	-
Available for use	1000	1000	1500	2000	2500
Balance	1500	2000	2500	2500	2500

Note:
Funds available for use lags balances.
If payments are made when the balance is there but the funds are not available for use, fees are
often charged.

Source: IBS Publishing

Value dating is used heavily with paper-based items and foreign currency payments. To place value dating within some parameters, for cross-border payments the European Union requires banks to make payments within an agreed time frame (five working days), after which a bank's customer can ask for compensation. Especially around foreign drafts (paper payment orders), banks, often give a three-week estimate and point out that the fees involved to process a foreign cheque may be substantial. The bank handling the paper in the country upon which the cheque or draft is drawn may also add an additional fee. Any cheque or draft from one country to another for less than $25 is probably going to be worth very little when going through the collection process, which involves administration charges.

Often a bank sees the transactions that are value dated and often allows transactions through based on the relationship with the customer.

Figure 9.7: Value dated transactions

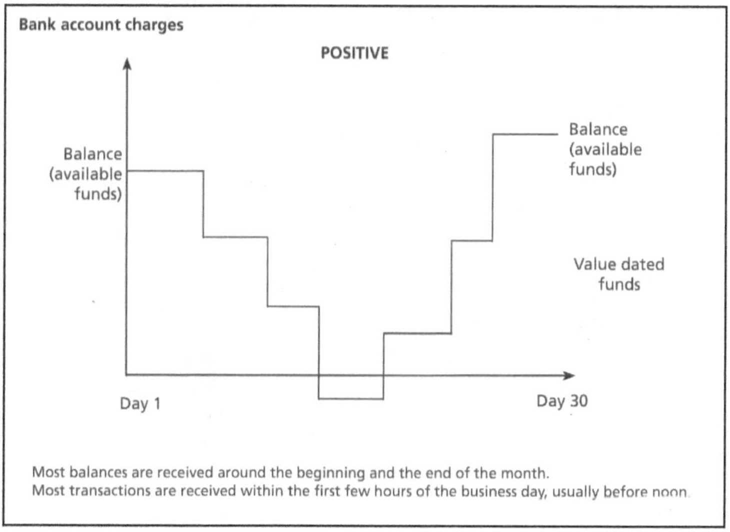

Source: IBS Publishing

International payments for businesses

Correspondent banking payments

As a company moves into international cash management, it needs a bank to support its business across countries. In banking this used to be the 'International Department' connected to their correspondent bank.

Correspondent banking was a very profitable business until electronic banking arrived. The move from manual to electronic cost money and reduced the time the bank held onto the money. Hence, there are many fewer banks with electronic international cash management than those offering domestic cash management, as many domestic banks did not make the necessary changes. In one way, for a domestic bank, it was an easy decision to make not to provide international cash management, as most countries have less than 2% of their payments made internationally.

Instead of being routed through a domestic company bank account, foreign exchange payments should be made through the company's account in that country.

Figure 9.8: Foreign exchange payments

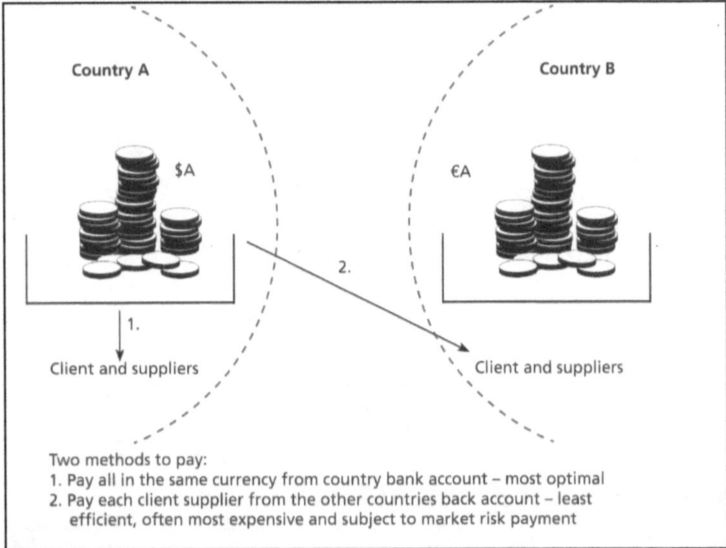

Source: IBS Publishing

Other international payment options

This relationship can be made either by the company directly – the most time-consuming – or through their domestic bank, usually their correspondent bank or through a domestic bank in an international association e.g. IBOS Association, or directly through an international bank.

Both options are limited to the areas covered by the Association or international bank. For example, Equens, a European bank-owned organisation based in the Netherlands, handled €9.7 billion payment transactions and 3.9 billion Point of Sale (POS) and ATM transactions in 2010, yet only covers a small group of countries.

The best option is to have connected banks making international bank transfers across in-bank accounts. In other words, if a company uses the same bank in two countries then a growing number of international banks will permit money transfers between accounts regardless of location as they are held within the same internal infrastructure.

Figure 9.9: Options for international payments – independent domestic banks

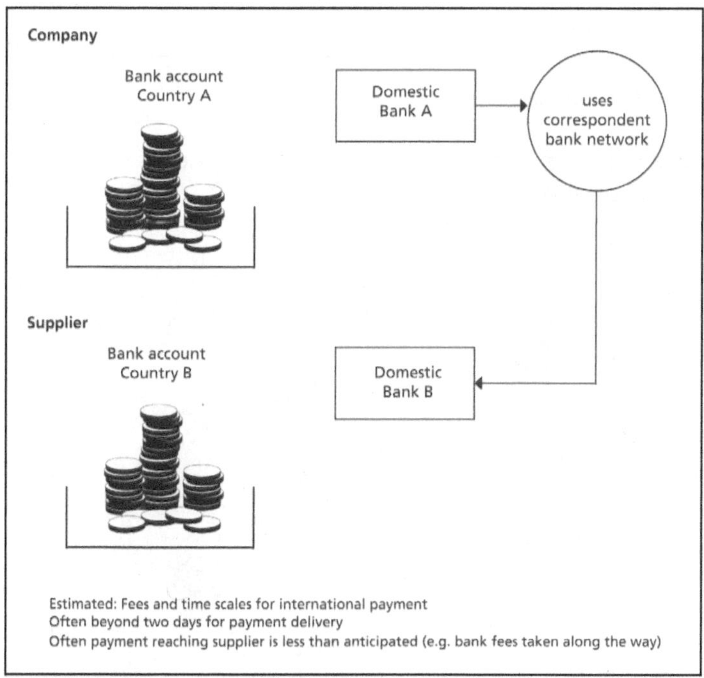

Source: IBS Publishing

Figure 9.10: Options for international payments – domestic banks in an Association

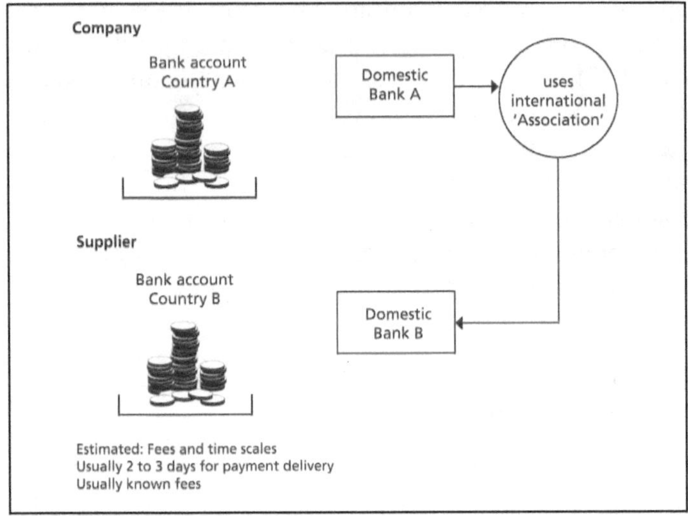

Source: IBS Publishing

Figure 9.11: Options for international payments – international bank

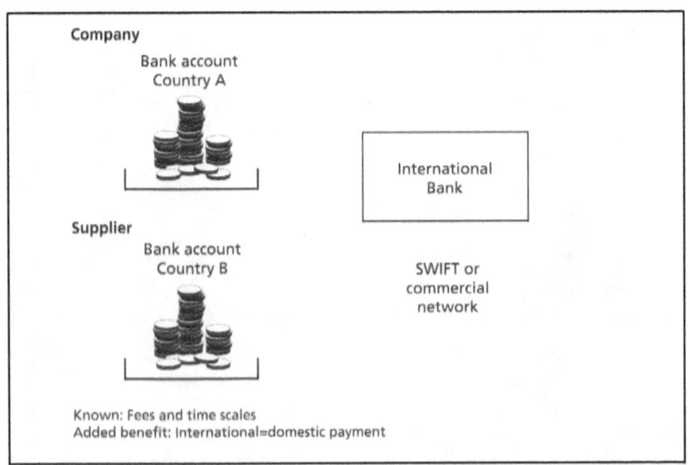

Source: IBS Publishing

The banking infrastructure for cross-border payments

The traditional banking infrastructure for cross-border payments has typically involved four banks. These are the bank of the payer, its correspondent bank, and the bank of the biller and its correspondent bank.

Figure 9.12: Traditional cross-border payments

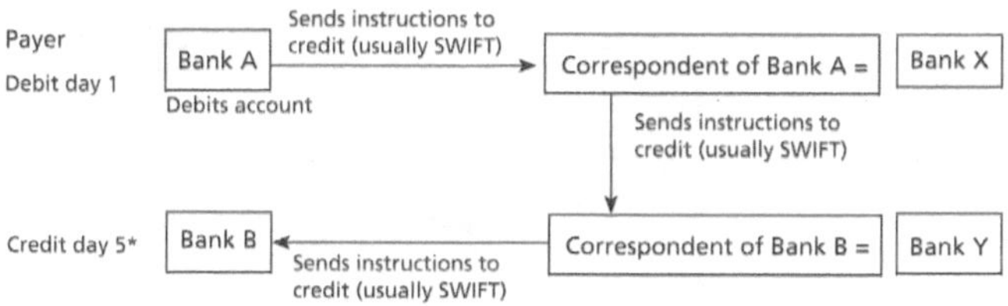

Source: Author

The correspondent banking system is well established worldwide and the infrastructure of many institutions only permits this type of routing. SWIFT was initially established to bring standard formats and telecommunication to international payments.

Third party account managers

Third party account managers can use any form of payment. The one that is most used is the DD for collecting money at source and paying the recurring bills. By adding an 8-digit customer reference number to the incoming or exiting DD (complete with the IBAN and BIC of the third party) the payment flows through the process automatically. On request for payment of a DD, the requestor's reference number is added.

Figure 9.13: Direct debit to a virtual account

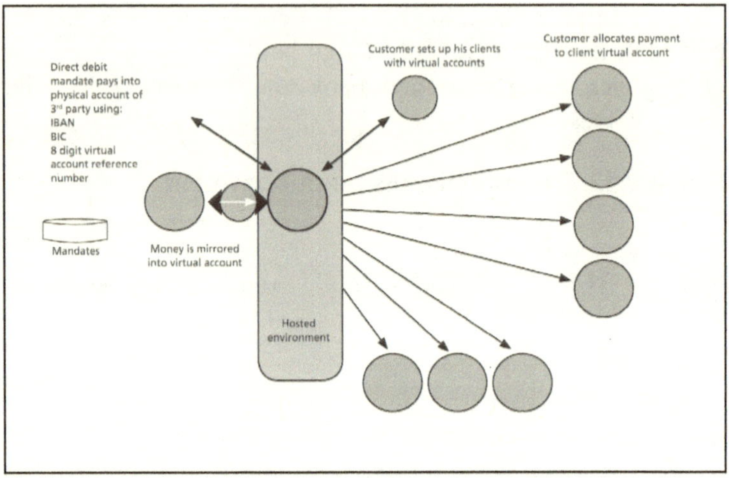

Direct debit
mandate pays into
physical account of
3rd party using:
IBAN
BIC
8 digit virtual
account reference
number
Mandates
Money is mirrored
into virtual account
Hosted
environment
Customer sets up his clients
with virtual accounts
Customer allocates payment
to client virtual account

Source: Author

Figure 9.14: Direct debit from a virtual account

Direct debit
mandate requests
payment from
client of 3rd party
using:
IBAN
BIC
8 digit virtual
account reference
number
Mandates
Direct debit is
paid or rejected
by 3rd party
from the client's
virtual account
Payment message
shows payee's:
IBAN
BIC
Payee's reference
numbers
Money is
mirrored
into virtual
account
Hosted
environment
3rd Party monitors request
Client's direct
debit requests
payment
Balance is checked
Balance cannot
cover the request;
the request
is rejected
Balance can cover
the amount; the
request is paid

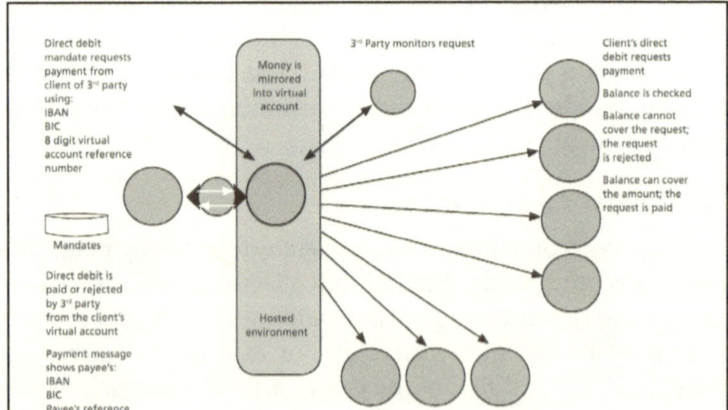

Source: Author

Payment fees

Transaction fees charged by banks may be explicit (a known amount per each kind of transaction), or implicit (dependent on the overall relationship with the bank). The more banking services are used, the lower the fees charged. Each bank sets its own rates. In Europe, payment fees are limited by law to encourage market price stability and prevent excess fees being charged.

In correspondent banking payment it is often commonplace for each bank in the chain to take a fee. This has also been addressed by the EU, which allows the originator to pay all the fees along the payment path, instead of the beneficiary receiving less money due to fees being deducted.

Transactions for warehousing are usually based as a percentage of the amount transferred into the warehouse that can vary from 2.5% to 5%. Once the money is in the warehouse, additional explicit fees for transferring the money to other accounts can be levied. PayPal, for example, charges a percentage of the amount ranging from 3.4% for £1,500 per month dropping down to 1.4% for over £55,000 per month, plus a transaction charge of £0.2.

Based on the level of transactions and the cost a bank account can be compared to a warehouse account. A basic bank account is needed to provide funds into a warehouse account. The advantage of the warehouse account is the money is moved same day between countries. The disadvantage is the company or person you are sending money to or expect money from needs a warehouse account.

Table 9.2: Comparison of bank and warehouse account pricing

	Bank account		Warehouse account	
	Cost/ month	**Transaction fee**	**Cost/ month**	**Transaction fee**
Basic	£0.00		0	
Package	£15.00			
Transactions				2.50%
CHAPS		£25.00		
Faster payments		£0.30		
ACH		£0.30		
Cheques		£0.30		
International (EU)		£0.80		
Outside EU		£15.00		

Cost of bank vs. warehouse account			
Money moved in a month	**Bank**	**Warehouse**	**Assumptions**
£500.00	£16.50	£12.50	5 transactions
£1,000.00	£18.80	£25.00	10 transactions + 1 EU
£2,500.00	£21.00	£62.50	20 + 2 EU + 1 Outside EU
£5,000.00	£36.80	£125.00	50+ 1 EU + 1 Outside EU
£10,000.00	£79.00	£250.00	100 + 10 EU + 2 Outside EU
£50,000.00	£241.00	£1,250.00	200 + 20 + 10
£100,000.00	£429.00	£2,500.00	300 + 30 + 20

Bank accounts vs. warehouse accounts cost summary		
	Account balance	**Equal to each other occurs at**
Money movement	£500.00	3.30%
	£1,000.00	1.88%
	£2,500.00	0.84%
	£5,000.00	0.74%
	£10,000.00	0.79%
	£50,000.00	0.48%
	£100,000.00	0.43%

The rise in packaged accounts in the UK and the charging of payments for the SME has led to a narrowing of the cost between operating a basic bank account for free and using the warehouse account to pay away money. At a 2.5% levy it is cheaper to use a warehouse account than a bank account for under £1,000 cash through a month. For amounts up to £12,500 per month the warehouse account fees need to be around 1%, provided the account is being used mainly domestically. The more international transfers are made – they cost £15 per time outside the EU – the better the pricing of the warehouse account looks.

Europe – legal timeliness

As of January 2012 all euro transaction legally need to occur within D+1 (Day 1 plus another business day maximum allowed) By 2010 all banks in the EU were capable of processing incoming SEPA Direct Debits.

The EU Parliament has set the end date for SEPA Direct Debits to be in place by February 2014. The EU's legally binding date is to ensure EU-wide rules to make the payment service fair, eliminate hidden charges, and accelerate transfers. In doing so, this could save as much as €123 billion across the European economy within six years. All the banks will finally be able to receive and send SEPA Direct Debits.

A pull mechanism operates for SMEs with clients taking a regular service. The money can now be taken across Europe from any customer permitting a direct debit.

The level of domestic cash management sophistication and services offered is determined by a country's approach to the rules and regulations surrounding payments and the competition to banks themselves. Outside SEPA, the terms and conditions of payments are determined at the country level. For example, certain countries, for example Australia, are considering SEPA-like standards.

Credit cards

Credit card usage within businesses and financial institutions is on the rise, but still represents only a small part of cash management. The banks are the major issuers, acquirers and members of the major network brands (Visa, MasterCard and American Express). The companies in turn have added debit and prepaid cards to their network brand payment solutions mix. These can assist businesses where collection or disbursement of small amounts of cash is needed. The credit card process has its own structure, as follows.

Credit card process cycle – key plavers

Like any payment scheme, there are a number of parties involved. Let's start with the credit card holder making a purchase.

Figure 9.15: The credit card process cycle

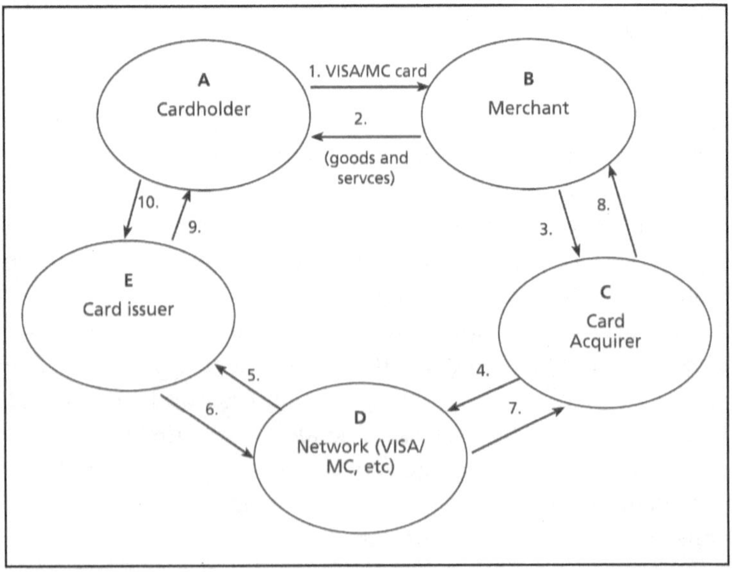

Source: Author

Sample transaction and stakeholders

A. *Cardholder makes a credit card purchase (step 1) and pays for it at step 10 of the cycle*

The time between purchase and payment can be up to 56 days and with no interest charged if paid in full. Interest charges on the balances after that time can vary up to 35%. In Canada, for example, the average fee is 19.99%

B. *Merchant provides goods and services to the cardholder (step 2) and receives payment from the card acquirer (step 8)*

The time between the merchant sending in the transactions for payment and receiving payment is a negotiation between the merchant and the card acquirer, usually 28 days. The fees are usually between 1.5 –5%; for example the Canadian Competition Bureau in 2009 reported 1.5–3% with the premium card brand, for example MasterCard Premium, at the top end of the pricing. As cardholders can reject transactions up to nine months after purchase for immediate credit, acquirers often hold back payment from the merchant as a cash cushion. Cash cushions can often reach 10% of the merchant's turnover. In addition, new merchants may see reduced payments until the cash cushion has reached acquirer acceptable levels. Merchants in the higher risk categories often pay in excess of 5% transaction fees.

C. *Card acquirer sends transactions into the network provider (Visa, MasterCard and American Express are the main ones) (step 4) and the network provider pays the acquirer (step 7) less interchange fees*

The network provider pays the acquirer on terms; both the timeliness and fees are usually in the rulebook of the network provider. Visa and MasterCard have sub-second processing speeds per transaction of 20 and 47 milliseconds respectively

D. *The network forwards the transactions onto the card Issuer (step 5) and receives payment for them (step 6)*

The network provider has a set of rules including fees by which both the issuer and acquirer must abide, otherwise they could lose their membership.

E. *The issuer invoices the cardholder (step 9) and receives payment or query from the cardholder (step 10)*

In its 2010 annual report, Visa Europe noted gains in the commercial card business of 10%, which increased the number of cards to 12.4 million per year. While this is less than 5% of the total cards issued (Visa issued 408 million) the corporate did charge €61 billion in the year.

On direct debit cards, Visa reached agreement with the European Commission in relation to cross-border interchange fees for immediate debit card payments based on the 'Merchant Indifference Test'. The cross-border direct debit card transaction fee is set at 0.2% per item. Visa regards deferred debit and credit transactions as more comparable to other instruments that provide a line of credit, as opposed to cash and cheque.

Using credit cards as working capital for SMEs

A report by Warwick Business School in February 2012 showed that in the UK:

- SMEs spend £1.8 billion on their business credit cards every month;
- 12% of corporate cards were used to buy equipment and vehicles;
- SMEs' average usage for working capital was:
  - 55% business credit cards;
  - 53% had overdrafts;
  - 24% used term loans;
  - 3% per cent used equity finance;
- Level of debt rolled over:

  - SMEs pay 95% of the credit card debt when due;
- UK SME characteristics:
  - SMEs use the major banks (HSBC, Lloyds TSB, Barclays and Royal Bank of Scotland) 82% of the time in England and Wales and 95% in Scotland;
  - Few SMEs change banks - just 2% each year;
  - 33% express dissatisfaction with their bank charges (on average £51 per month);
  - 29% would move if approached by another financial provide;r
  - SMEs' average term loan is £88,000.

Cash cushions

However, there is a need for SMEs to have a safety net against short-term problems, according Warwick University's report. The report showed SMEs have a total of £4 billion net positive cash position. This is made up of £92bn in total deposits and £88 billion owed in loans.

The use of credit cards and the fees involved in the SME sector are universal. Take as examples Australia and Bangladesh.

Australia

In Australia, strong credit card usage by SMEs helped push Australian credit card debt to a record $50 billion in November 2011. East & Partners says business likely comprised about $14 billion – or almost 30% – of the total spending. The reason is because SMEs are turning to credit cards amid difficulties accessing traditional debt funding over the past few years. East & Partners noted: "We see a lot of cash flow-based credit card usage by small business. And although interest rates being charged are pretty horrendous, they seem to use credit cards almost as a default way of accessing short-term credit."

In the past five years, Australia's credit card debt has grown 30%. Contrarily, Australia's savings rate is at a two-decade high; this is largely due to concern over the global financial outlook.

Bangladesh

In February 2012 the Central Bank of Bangladesh asked the commercial banks to maintain a spread between average deposit rate and lending rate up to 5% for all types of loans, except high-risk consumer loans, including credit card, and SME loans. A spokesman noted: 'The central bank has authorised the banks to set their interest rates for SME sector, as loans for the sector are collateral-free and thus risky."

The CBB directive means that if any bank's average deposit rate is 10%, it cannot charge more than 15% interest on lending for all sectors, excepting consumer and SME loans. The official noted that banks were already charging around 17.50-20% interest on SME loans. That is a spread of 7.5 to 10%.

Prepaid cards

Prepaid usage was first driven by expatriates, the unbanked, migrant workers, credit deprived people, gift-giving and loyalty cards. The use of prepaid mobile phones was a key promoter and educator of the concept. The sharing of the fees between the banks and the telecommunication companies led to the ability to top up the mobile phone account at ATMs.

Prepaid cards are offered by the major card scheme providers (Visa, MasterCard, etc) to their customers; customers can put money on a card and dispatch that card to the recipient. The recipient can then use the card at ATMs and POS worldwide. The card can be used until the amount loaded onto it is used up. There are two types of card – disposal and reloadable. The disposables are thrown away once used. The reloadables, like 'pay as you go' mobiles, can have new money added at any time. Table 9.3 shows typical prepaid card charges.

Table 9.3 Prepaid card fees

Account set-up	Free to £30	One time
Monthly	Free to £15	Per month
Transaction	Free to 3%	Per request for authorisation
ATM	0.5% to 3%	Per £100 taken
Internet purchases	Free to 3%	Per purchase
Overdraft charges	Free to 30%	Monthly fees; request for transactions are tracked and deducted when new money is added to the card

Source: Author

There can be many different types of pricing, and the permutations are many. The Canadian Financial Consumer Agency, an independent government financial watchdog, described prepaid products as "an expensive way to spend your own money".

In 2011 Visa noted that if growth in prepaid and debit transactions continues, it could account for more than half of Visa's global purchases business in the next five years. The possibilities for the introduction of prepaid are vast; at the moment, there are even incentives being developed whereby the prepaid card system can be used on a mobile phone to purchase something like coffee. The retail sector can offer prepaid cards to their customers. Loyalty schemes implemented through the prepaid cards can bring in cash now and retain the customer. For example, Starbucks estimates that 25% of purchases in the US are now completed using its prepaid loyalty card.

One of the most popular uses of prepaid card is the travel card. Here the card is loaded with different foreign currencies. It is a win-win for all. The provider makes the fees through the FX spread, the corporate can see what and where their money and exposures are, and the user can access cash and make payments in local currencies.

SMEs can keep bank costs low when it comes to transferring their employee's wages onto a prepaid card. So instead of cheques or waiting on bank transfers, employees of SMEs can have their funds made available immediately and with the standard Visa access.

For an SME with international activities, the funding of small, local activities can be done through a prepaid card. As prepaid is competing against cash, a business using a pooled prepaid account can move the cash virtually immediately across to those accounts that need it. Control of internal staff expenses can be improved and the resulting paperwork decreased. In addition, management information on where the money is going and how it is being spent is available electronically. Using prepaid at the right fees has its advantages for a business. Banks are beginning to offer prepaid services as part of their suite of cash management offerings.

Near Field Communication (NFC) payments

NFC is a high frequency application allowing exchange of data between devices that are less than 20 centimetres apart, often referred to as contactless payment. An international standard has been established (ISO/IEC 14443) and the need today is to establish an infrastructure within which NFC can be readily used. The mobile phone market is a strong backer of this technology and in the UK the four major networks – Orange, O2, T-Mobile and Vodaphone – are NFC-compliant.

NFC payments often referred to as 'tap and go' and come in two forms – closed or open loop. An example of a closed system is payment for public transportation. Here entry to that system is by physical POS devices and a prepaid NFC-compliant card created by the carrier. An open system is one in which the NFC-compliant prepaid, debit or credit card or mobile phone can be used anywhere. One example of this is 2012 Olympics, where Visa, LloydsTSB and Samsung are provided preloaded credit for the athletes and officials. The Visa contactless payment option is called Payway; MasterCard's is called PayPass.

Reconciliation

It is well understood by financial professionals that profitable businesses fail every day if cash flow is negative and the 2008 credit crunch brought this home to even the largest conglomerates such as GE that had borrowed short and was unable to roll over credit lines. Most corporate Treasurers and CFOs don't have the luxury that GE had of tapping into emergency funding programs such as TARP and have to rely on their bank.

In the UK, after bailing out the banks, the government insisted the banks lent money to the SME market under 'Project Merlin'. The Bank of England's official assessment of Project Merlin found that lending to small businesses was £74.9 billion, £1.1 billion short of the target. Credit lines are being squeezed and overdraft rates are up, so understanding the numbers has never been more important. Bank of England Governor Sir Mervyn King in February 2012 spoke against the "harsh treatment" of small and medium companies being starved of the funds they need to grow, create jobs and drive the economic recovery. Bank of England figures show that net lending fell by £10.7 billion in 2011 – in other words, the banks received £10.7 billion more in loan repayments than they gave out in new loans. That took the total fall in credit outstanding since the end of 2008 to £82.7 billion.

Reconciliations are the end of a long process which may have been strung out over a number of months and include winning an order, receiving a purchase order, delivering of the goods/services, issuing an invoice and receiving a payment without having to chase for payment. The final step often gets less focus, as payment has now been received and typically staff that carry out reconciliations have many other duties which are more visible to their colleagues and are often prioritised as more urgent.

Timely, accurate reconciliations are vital part of the process because:

- Business decisions lean heavily on accurate financial decisions;
- Credit control processes can only be activated with confidence once unrecognised items have accounted ;
- Fraud (in-house or by customers) can be identified (and deterred) by timely reconciliation of ledgers and bank accounts;
- Incorrect bank charges, fees, interest or FX conversions can be identified and addressed early –, it can be a significant amount of work to recalibrate the books if there is a long-standing error that has not been identified;
- Regulations are obligations that if left undiscovered can lead to significant fines –
  - PwC failed to notice that JP Morgan Securities Ltd had not properly segregated an average of $8.6 billion of client funds from the firm's accounts; the UK FSA fined the bank $33.3 million pounds in 2010;
  - The FSA fined Towry Investment Management Ltd £494,000 for providing misleading information to the FSA and client money breaches. The FSA set out clear rules on how firms need to treat client money in its Client Asset Sourcebook (CASS).

Reconciliation is often one of the last functions to be done on a timely basis as it often compared to looking for needles in haystacks. It is also time-consuming, costly and boring with often little gain in terms of value for money. Most reconciliations result in less than 10% errors. However, those 10% or fewer errors could be a high-risk business, especially when those needles turn out to be unmatched payments, internal fraud or payments applied to the wrong account which, when reversed, open up a negative black hole. It's common that the favourable cash position is often with one of the worst payers.

As volumes of payment traffic grow, the chances of mismatched transactions occurring increase. To offset these chances without automation of the process requires additional administration in terms of people to resource the reconciliation process. Reconciliation of the bank accounts to that of the business back office helps prevent losses in financial and customer service terms. No-one, especially the regulators, likes to see payments not recorded against the right account and for the right amount.

The issue is the historic information structure that surrounds the early days of the Automatic Clearing Houses (ACHs). Many ACH payments have limited remittance information that can be forwarded to the beneficiary due to the 18-character remittance advice field started when electronic payments begin. A beneficiary receiving the limited remittance information cannot apply the funds automatically without first finding the customer and then the invoice being credited. Often the remitter's reference number is shortened or not present at all. The payer often has not included it its payment details or has transcribed them wrong. Just ask British Telecoms (BT) as they try and post similar amounts across their millions of clients. There are also complications in terms of fees and charges by the bank, the addition of interest and with foreign exchange, and the rates being used pre- and post-correction.

To overcome these issues, reconciliation should take place is daily and be as highly automated as possible. The process should highlight only the exceptions (usually less than 10% of the volume but often representing 80% of the cost) and suggest matches through business intelligence built into the process. For example:

- Highlight possible matches;
- Traces by source;
- Multi to one and one to multi entries possible matches;
- Automating accounting entries for correction (with dual sign-off)

The automation reduces the cost of administration and customer service is much improved. The need for further automation is clearly reflected in a survey from the Aberdeen Group in April 2011, where 29% of companies had fully automated the procedure to pay (accounts payable – A/P) and 25% of companies had fully automated the order to cash (accounts receivable – A/R).

Those companies who had automated the A/P and A/R noted:

1. Processing of Day Sales Outstanding (DSO) dropped to 21 days versus the industry average of 53 days; and
2. Cash flow forecast rate was 84% accurate as compared to the industry average of 49%.

That is, by performing best practice it is clear the organisation benefits. The areas that should be focused on are as follows.

Table 9.4: The reconciliations process

	Today	Future
Process	1. Manual – paper-based (storage, future referencing) 2. Complexities – errors (self-compensating errors) with no systematic priorities 3. Administratively expensive, boring work flow – ideal for inertia and mismanagement 4. Data taken out of secure systems (in-house fraud risk and additional audit checks required)	1. Automated 2. Exception management and prioritisation – degrees of difficulty and amount size 3. Automated workflows showing segregation and timing of changes – time stamps, full audit trail 4. Data held in secure and monitored environment making it harder to defraud
People and training	1. Low value activity, while important task, rarely seen as a priority 2. Problem solving people required, understanding the business and making the right decision. Often on the job training – sit with Nellie, stand with Sid	1. With reduced volumes and the right tools, less unskilled work required 2. Skilled people to get to the bottom of the problems quickly rather than waiting for escalation with suggested online solutions
Ownership	1. Low grade administrative with limited escalation unless a crisis	1. Moving up organisation often to board level as liquidity is paramount – accurate cash forecasting and liquidity management are increasing in important
Technology	1. Fantastic technology used today, Excel spreadsheets – now what numbers would management like! 2. Macros can help, colour coding etc 3. Format and flat files (pre-defined rigid structures) – now where is that tub file filed with paper ledgers?	1. Real time updating – link e-banking to internal automated systems, installed or through cloud technology 2. Splits out fees, charges, interest into separate items, FX – midpoint days rate versus actual 3. e-invoicing and XML
Metrics – measure it to manage it	1. List common metric e.g. DSOs outstanding prepared manually before reconciliation 2. Reconciliation timeliness is often monthly or even quarterly	1. List common metric e.g. DSOs outstanding reported after reconciliation Reconciliation timeliness is daily
Ownership	1. List common metric e.g. DSOs outstanding prepared manually before reconciliation 2. Reconciliation timeliness is often monthly or even quarterly	1. List common metric e.g. DSOs outstanding reported after reconciliation Reconciliation timeliness is daily

Reconciliation is the last stage of the payment process. One reason it is not automated is that, while everyone acknowledges that is very important, the resources needed within the business are frequently working on higher prioritised activities. The need to automate is critical to give an internal closer and more timely view of the monies collected and paid. What prevents the automation is the paper process; the lack of standards around invoices and the number of ways payments can be gathered and sent.

The future

Same-day electronic payment from a personal or smartphone for one-off payments will become the norm over time. Similarly, the receipt of recurring payments such as payroll will be via direct debit.

For banks, this is a crisis. They lose float and will fight the movement to shorter timeframes. Only regulators and legal provisions such as the European Directive of payment by D+1 will overcome the resistance.

For SMEs, electronic payments are best, particularly because of receiving the money on the same day, and will become commonplace. With e-invoicing, the payment wait between performing the service or buying a product and getting paid can happen the same day. Same-day payments are irrevocable, so payments are received with certainty that the obligations have been settled.

For SMEs paying out money to their suppliers could result in them acting like a bank – i.e. is holding onto their suppliers' money for as long as possible. This tendency has to be resisted, as governments and regulators may turn their attention away from the banks to the business market. The cost of future compliance is far more than following best practice now. Fast payments creates economic velocity which in turn brings economic growth.

Cheques will continue to drop in volume as immediate payments and direct debits programs remove much of the need for paper. SMEs receiving cheques should request electronic payments; similarly, the SME writing cheques should look to change to electronic payment.

SMEs can go back to 'cash on the barrelhead'. No more waiting around for payment; if the person has a smartphone, they can download the appropriate app and make payment immediately.

CHAPTER 10
FOREIGN EXCHANGE

Questions for SME directors

- Who is looking after the foreign exchange, and is it done using the internet or through the bank, and how do we establish the rates?
- Have we taken out hedging positions against the major currency exposures?
- How is our domestic currency performing?
- Has anyone looked at the historic rates we have been charged against market rates at that time, given the spreads can exceed 10% in many currencies?
- Which currencies with the potential for appreciation should be maintained for payment?

Key considerations

- Considering foreign exchange options;
- Managing currency exposure;
- Using automated FX dealing;
- Monitoring currency movements, particularly Euro and USD appreciation and depreciation against a group of currencies.

International cash management and FX

WITH INTERNATIONAL CASH MANAGEMENT, the level of complexity increases dramatically. Also, a particular bank's business customers' commitment to the international arena is reflected in the level of commitment towards international cash management. Large businesses can have significant influence over what services their local banks provide. The reason is, like any good service provider, the bank wants to meet the specific needs of its clients.

The first sign of international cash management is foreign exchange. Companies often price their services in their home currencies, putting the onus on the buyer to sort out the currency risks. Others price in their home currency and one other major currency, which is often USD or euros.

Most banks offer a FX 'branch' rate, usually up to amounts up to $50,000 for transactions from one currency to another. The rate is changed once a day and contains a substantial spread, often 6% (depending on currency) either side of the mid-point market rate, plus a transaction fee.

FX rates for a pair of currencies are now easy to establish using the internet. Some businesses' internal policies insist on three quotes. The main function of the business is to make payments and these tend to occur at the end of the month.

Managing foreign exchange options

Cash management goes international once a company starts buying or selling a product or service continuously involving a second currency. Now there is another currency to be tracked, measured and valued in the cash flow.

Effective management of foreign currency risk stabilises the company's performance. Currency risk management programmes can structure a cost-effective currency management strategy to match the risk exposure. A comprehensive set of currency management services would include derivatives, spot, forward and options contracts.

e-options

The ability to purchase options is becoming easier with banks and others offering e-options. The price of the option is derived from the difference between the reference price and the value of the underlying asset, plus a premium based on the time remaining until the expiration of the option. See Table 10.1.

Table 10.1: Example of currency option pricing based on basis point spread

Currency		1 month	3 months
Against GBP	Mid point of currency	Option Premium added (Basis point spread)	Option
Euro	8.90	5	15
US	1.55	5	14
Japan	119.70	9	32

Source: The Times, 31 December 2011

Regulatory changes

The derivative market is undergoing extensive regulatory changes, as at the height of the market, derivatives traders overestimated the liquidity available and failed to acknowledge that companies would default on the obligations. Derivatives issued on OTC (Over the Counter) are being repositioned onto an exchange-based system that will bring more transparency to this trillion-dollar market.

The Office of the Controller in the US reported in the 1st quarter 2011 that 1,047 insured US commercial banks reported derivative activities. The activity is concentrated in five banks, which represent 96% of the total banking industry notional accounts and 83% of the industry net currency exposure. Derivatives remain concentrated in interest rate products that comprise 82% of total derivative notional values; credit derivatives represent 6.1% of total derivatives notions of $14.9 trillion.

Other options

Forwards

Forwards are a way to manage exchange rate risks or to make payments of foreign currency payments that are needed in the future. Forward transactions enable the buying or selling of a currency at a fixed rate on a specified future date. By linking this date to the date of the currency payment, the future exchange rate is locked and eliminates the risk of further volatility in that transaction.

Interest rate swaps

Interest rate swaps are used when a company is borrowing in foreign currency and may want to manage its exposure to fluctuations in interest rates in that currency. An interest rate swap allows management of mix of fixed- and floating-rate debt synthetically, without the need to refinance.

Currency exposure

It is essential to cover future currency movements – as soon as the order is placed in another country, book an FX forward to cover the amount payable or due. For example, if one is buying steel from the US for delivery in the UK in six months' time, a six-month forward which sets the FX exchange rate can be bought. In six months' time, regardless of the USD and GBP exchange rate fluctuations, the margins on the steel contract remain intact. The cost of the steel is the same as it was six months ago. If the price of the pound had strengthened, the steel would be cheaper; similarly, if the USD had strengthened, the steel would cost more.

Once a company has two or more bank accounts in different currencies currency exposure is created, as any two currencies are rarely static over their values of exchange at any particular time. The market establishes its own value of a particular currency and changes can be dramatic. Every company has a statuary currency – its home currency – in which accounting and audit reports have to be filled. Consequently, accounts in a currency other than the statuary currency have to be shown, usually under the term 'currency exposure'.

Currency exposure can affect the profit and loss account, especially if there is a major currency movement both up or down; the value of international assets; the risk in long-term international contracts; sales revenues; borrowings in international currencies; and the timing of payments being made and received.

Here a rolling schedule of incoming fees and expenses in various currencies can show where the market risk is at its strongest. Trading with a country that has consistently high inflation often results in lower net revenues coming out of that country due to the difference in exchange rates. A country such as Australia, in dealing with the UK has seen its currency rise in terms of what the UK pound can buy. Hence, if income is coming out of Australia, the revenue is increased, but if costs are being incurred there these too will increase.

Buying and selling FX

There are a couple of ways to ensure the exposure is well-managed and the cash needed in the future is predictable.

The currency rate quotes have two figures – the buy price and the sell price. The mid rate is often quoted, giving an idea of the currency value as judged by the market at that particular time. Currencies can become volatile and can move upwards or downwards of 5% in a day. The currencies themselves are divided into prime, secondary and tertiary (exotic) currencies. The prime currencies are the most liquid, e.g. USD, and the tertiary are the least, e.g. Kenyan Shilling. The US dollar is the world's currency of choice, with 50% of all trades having a dollar component. The margins, or gap, between the quoted buy and sell rates quoted also reflects the lack of liquidity in a particular currency.

Once a company moves to active from infrequent FX transactions then the bank, depending on the amounts involved, permit access to the 'Corporate FX desk' or introduce them to automated foreign exchange (e-trading). The FX desk is located on the trading room floor. This enables the company to buy or sell currencies at more favourable rates.

Through a dealer with a phone, a company can see and trade (execute) on a moving market FX rate (the rate is usually held for 30 seconds by the trading party) from an online FX service. These services are readily available through banks and non-banks. Often, local banks can brand an FX service from a major financial institution, with the market risk covered by that institution. The company, though, now has an exposure in another currency if it is not a straight one-off payment.

Credit line from the bank

The key to buying and selling FX is a credit line limit from the bank. The reason is the settlement process that governs the surrounding currency movement. A spot trade in a currency takes two days to settle. In that time, the currency purchased can increase or decrease in value. The risk is that one leg of the currency may not occur on time, or if a bank fails, not at all. The risk of a bank failing has been greatly reduced by Continuous Linked Settlement (CLS). A consortium of banks owns CLS with governance under the Federal Reserve in the US. CLS has reduced this risk to banks across a range of currencies. This in turn safeguards the client's customers.

Spread and commission-based pricing

Some traders prefer trading on commissions over spread based trading, and, sometimes, the other way around. Clients often mention the fact that commission-based pricing allows them to get a better feeling for the markets' price action, while others prefer all costs of trading to be included in the Bid/Ask quote, as this may be more transparent.

Automated FX (e-trading)

According to *Euromoney*, the multi-bank and independent platforms are growing rapidly and now handling $48 trillion a year in foreign currency value.

To begin automated trading of FX the retailer needs the money being traded to be in an account with them. Similar to the warehouse payment movement money is transferred into an account under the FX providers' authority. Once money has been put into that account then the client is ready to buy and sell currencies.

Today, clients are often given prices off the same pricing feed. A pricing feed is the capture of the price of a currency in real time and offered to a client electronically. The major price feeds for the full range of currencies are provided by the larger global banks. Vendors such as Reuters and Bloomberg provide rate information on screens. The global bank price feeds are used as the wholesaler price. Vendors and the smaller banks take the major price feeds and offer them to their clients.

The banks provide the currency prices with a built-in spread. The retailer aggregates the clients' amounts and when a currency amount has been reached and the credit lines established with the global bank, a trade is executed. The vendor or bank then gives the trade to the global bank to trade that currency back into the currency of the home currency. This gives the retailer limited to virtually no exposure to the market. The positions being created by the aggregation of the smaller trades are covered once they reach a certain size, and as such, do not expose the retailer to suffering major market shifts in the wrong direction.

Currency movements

Margin, or increased leverage

The retailer can provide the client with a margin account that enables the client to buy more currency than he has in the account. The reason for this is that the retailer is looking at the movement that particular currency is making in a day. It is rare for a major or secondary currency to move by 10% in any one day. Consequently, the retailer with the authorisation over the account can sell out that currency when required should the money in the account not be sufficient to pay if the rates move downwards.

Depending on the retailer, the client's profile and the past practices, the following margins can be issued for a major currency:

- Assuming 10% daily historic movement, the retailer could give a margin of 10 to 1. That means the client can buy 10 times the amount in the account. By putting in £1,000 into the account, the client can buy £10,000. The retailer probably has a stop-loss order.
- Assuming a 2.5% daily historic movement, the retailer could give a margin of 40 to 1. That means the £1,000 becomes £40,000.

In setting the margin for the account, the retailer takes into consideration the currency pair and the currency in the account.

A client could have the account in GBP and bought EUR and sold USD. The client could be looking for short-term gains and closing out the position at the end of the day. This way, no market risk is taken overnight.

Comparing euro performance

Taking a view over the last two years of market trading of the euro's performance against other currencies, Table 11.2 shows the Australian Dollar, Chinese RMB, Swedish Kroner, USD and GBP rose 20%, 15.57%, 12.93% 9.7% and 5.68% respectively. Poland's currency, on the other hand, declined 8% in value. That means the euro could buy 8% more goods in Poland that in 2009, whereas goods from Australia cost 20% more.

Consequently, if any surplus cash were kept in either the Australian or Chinese currencies, a two-year appreciation of 20% and 15.67% over the euro would have been realised (less the currency exchange fees). In certain countries, the use of holding cash in currency other than the home currency is commonplace. An example of this is Zimbabwe where the US dollar is preferred over the local currency, which has lost most of its value over the last few years. In that period, the price of a car in local currency five years ago would now, five years later, buy a loaf of bread.

Table 10.2: Euro changes as reported by the European Central Bank

Currency	Dec-09	Dec-10	Dec-11	2 yr change	Largest daily Movements
Australia (AUD)	1.60	1.31	1.28	-20.00%	-2.40% 3.10%
Great Britain (GBP)	0.88	0.86	0.83	-5.68%	-1.80% 3.0%
USA (USD)	1.44	1.33	1.30	-9.72%	-2.70% 1.90%
Poland (PLN)	4.10	3.97	4.43	8.05%	-2.30% 3.10%
Sweden (Kroner)	10.29	8.96	8.96	-12.93%	-0.90% 1.10%
China (Renminbi - RMB)	9.83	8.82	8.29	-15.67%	-2.10% 1.90%

Asian currencies and the RMB

Traditionally, companies have kept their global cash surpluses in USD, EUR or GBP. This process is now undergoing a review, especially by those companies that see their Asian operations growing and becoming a larger part of their revenues and expenses. The Asian people have historically maintained far more currencies than those in the US and Europe. The reasons are often high interest rates in a particular currency and high inflation that in turn creates volatility of that currency. Most Asian bank accounts clients use five or more currencies, whereas in the US and Europe, the majority stays with one currency. The reason for reviewing the choice of an Asian currency is the chance of long-term appreciation.

The Chinese authorities are encouraging the RMB to be used as a settlement currency for international trades. With its deposits in RMB doubling in the last few years, Hong Kong is a major beneficiary of this policy, and has the largest offshore deposits of RMB in the world. A European Central Bank report shows the RMB has become a key driver of currency movements in Asia since the mid-2000s and even more so since the financial crisis. China's dominance in the region and the role of the RMB in the international monetary system makes it already a tri-polar currency; that is, the USD, EUR and RMB are now equally acceptable in the market.

The future

The FX market is one of the most transparent markets in the world, with price availability across the web. The next phase is the move to same-day payment or D+1 and the removal of spot timing of D+2 for the major currencies. Nordea provides this for the Nordic currencies today. The use of options will also become common as they become demystified and easier to purchase and monitor.

The banks will continue to dominate this space, as extra-large credit lines are needed to attract the trading volume. The trading volume will continue high as algorithmic trading (mathematical formulae that are aimed at predicting currency prices) becomes commonplace. Computers perform algo trading to take advantage of price differentials and trading trends. The greater the volume, the greater the chances of accurately forecasting which way the currency prices are heading.

SMEs will move the bulk of the currency trading to the web. This may be done through their bank, if the bank has online

FX on e-banking, or more likely, through an FX portal (a site dedicated to providing FX quotes and execution – an account is needed). Like banks, it is often best to have two. The two FX portals can then be viewed and compared with each other before trading.

SMEs holding more than one currency will have the capability to trade electronically at any time of the day. They will also actively manage the currencies through stop-loss orders.

CHAPTER 11
SUPPLY CHAIN MANAGEMENT

Questions for SME directors

- Are our accounts receivable and accounts payable automated; what is the aging and the amount expressed in terms of working capital at a 10% interest rate?
- How much of our receivables exceeds the agreed terms of our contracts and how can it be reduced?
- Does it make commercial sense to use invoice factoring to help cash flow?
- How many of our invoices received and sent are electronic?

Key considerations

- Automating the supply chain;
- Determining the size of the supply chain;
- Using various types of invoice financing;
- Moving to e-invoicing.

The supply chain and liquidity

THE SUPPLY CHAIN is often the SME's centre of business activity. The goal of supply chain management is to coordinate the movement of goods and services with the movement of money for the greatest efficiency.

The supply chain is full of potential to release liquidity for the parties involved. The best way to do this is to better understand the supply chain structure. Start by breaking down the process into the following components:

- Days Sales Outstanding (DSO) – the time it takes to collect payment once the service has been sold;
- Days Inventory Outstanding (DIO) – the time it takes to replenish the initial inventory;
- Days Payable Outstanding (DPO) – the time it takes to pay for the goods sold.

While all three can be influenced by the business, only DPO is fully controlled by the business. The goal is simply to reduced DSO and DIO by a third.

DPO

DPO often has a company guideline giving a sense of when the average payment will be made in terms of days lapsed. Many organisations, especially large ones, have service level agreements (SLAs) for payment, for example the National Health Service in the UK has promised to pay invoices within 30 days. Currently the NHS is achieving over 80% of its monthly accounts payables within 30 days of the invoice receipt.

DSO

DSO is often noted in credit reports as an indicator of the credit health of a company, a high level of old receivables outstanding viewed against the normal for that industry's sector could flag a concern. In addition, the older the receivables the less likely they will be fully collected.

Some Boards and/or management teams focus on DSO numbers, while others do not. One example of a change in management was in the international software sector Misys (UK FT250 company) had less than 40 days outstanding in 2005 and by 2011 this had grown to 86 days. The company mantra in the early 2000s was 'cash is king'; any receivables over 60 days were actively addressed and any receivable hitting 120 days were written off against the business. Today Misys has £69.4 million in trade receivables awaiting collection.

DIO

DIO is the working capital tied up in the inventory pending sales. The longer it takes to replenish the inventory, the longer it costs to fund. This is particularly the case in areas where tax and tolls are taken at the point of acceptance. For example, governments often put tax on alcohol, cigarettes and gas (petrol). This has lead to active inventory management especially if the tax is actively collected. In the UK, for example, the tax on petrol represents over 80% of the cost and as such most garages only carry one week's supply. Hence the 'just in time' methodology is being applied to non-manufacturing industries to save money and increase margins.

Supply chain management developments

The next major change in global cash management looks to be the electronic supply chain.

Financial supply chain innovation has tended to be bilateral, with a bank creating a specific solution for a customer without integrating the customer's trading partners. This is especially evident on the payable side, in which the buyer and the bank control the cash flows with relative ease. This approach does not permit the inclusion of others in the supply chain, which has been ably addressed by SWIFT's Trade Services Unit (TSU), especially since its the move to open accounts. Recent estimates suggest that more than 80% of global trade is now conducted on open account, moving away from the traditional forfaiting practices.

SWIFT's TSU

SWIFT's TSU is a centralised matching and workflow platform available to the SWIFT community. The platform provides timely and accurate comparison of data taken from underlying business purchase agreements and related documents, such as commercial invoices, transport and insurance.

The TSU supports the exchange of a 'Bank Payment Obligation' (BPO), an irrevocable conditional obligation from one bank to pay another bank, subject to the presentation of compliant data in the TSU. The "Notice of Intent to Pay" message is an additional information message indicating one company's intention to pay another company. Together, these two features provide a strong backbone for banks to offer alternative forms of financing, including pre-shipment, post-shipment and reverse factoring.

Forfaiting

Forfaiting (a French word meaning to surrender or relinquish the rights to something) enables a company to receive a cash payment on a without recourse basis and all risks associated with the transaction are transferred to the bank. The company receives immediate payment and surrenders the right to any further claim for payment. The benefits are:

- The receipt of cash upfront;
- The receivable is settled and removed from the balance sheet;
- All risks are removed including, sovereign, commercial bank, and corporate.

The bank providing the forfeiting makes certain the risks involved are covered and affects the transaction with one of the following debt instruments:

- Letter of Credit;
- Bills of Exchange;
- Promissory Notes;
- Standby Letters of Credit;
- Letter of Guarantee.

Forfaiting credit terms can vary from 90 days to 10 years, providing the underlying country and credit risks are acceptable. The minimum amount is $500,000 (or the equivalent in a major currency). Forfaiting is used extensively in Asia, with the most active markets being China, Korea, Japan, Taiwan and Indonesia.

Size of the supply chain

In 2011, REL Consultancy estimated there was $800 billion in 'trapped capital' in the US company supply chain That is money that a company may not know about and therefore is unable to reinvest or deploy to another part of the business. The 13th annual report by REL in July 2011 showed Europe's top 1,000 companies the following key changes from 2009 to 2010 showed:

Days Working Capital (DWC)	46.5 days in 2005 42.9 days in 2010 Improvement was 7.6%

DWC is composed of the accounts receivable added to the inventory and subtracting the accounts payable. This total is then divided by the total per day. (DWC = (A/R + Inventory – A/P)/(TotalRevenue/365)) and shows how many days it takes a company to convert its working capital into revenue. The faster it does this, the better the cash flow and efficiency of collecting money within the company. The shorter the working capital ratio, the better is the timeliness of the cash flow.

In 2010 SWIFT researchers Zanders' Report on Working Capital based on research on 4,127 companies worldwide from 10/2009 to 9/2010 from public reported financials estimated there was €3.67 trillion in trapped capital in the company supply chain. Since 2008, this has increased by €183.5 billion as debtors have slowed payments by 4.3 days of sale. In addition, Zanders found that:

- Asian companies had added 15 days to their funding from 2004 to 2010;
- Receivables and Inventory had increased to 88.5 days of sales;
- The above increase equated to €128.7 billion or 5% more liquidity needed.

In the US, the Aite Group research firm has shown that one of the top challenges for American companies is the need to move from paper to a fully automated process. In September 2011, it was estimated that nearly 60% of accounts payable were still paper-based.

Top 20% of companies achieve efficiencies

The Aberdeen Group in 2011 noted the same time period needed by the top 20% of companies could:

- Process an invoice from receipt through settlement in 5.3 days against the average of 10.2 days;
- Discounts for early payments were achieved in 60% of the time against the average of 9%;
- The average cost to process the invoice was $7.78 against the average of $12.05.

The common characteristics of the top 20% are:

- 3.8 x likely to establish pre-negotiated, fixed early discounts;
- 2.6 x likely to have automated alerts to notify managers of payments exceeding pre-defined thresholds;
- 1.4 x likely to have segmented their supply base for electronic payments.

The technology used across the process by the top 20% is:

Function	Usage by top 20%
Document imaging	56%
Electronic approval workflow	52%
Scanning	52%
Electronic bank account management	48%
Invoice networking	31%

The methodology used by 47% of the companies surveyed is paper and spreadsheets. 20% use internal Enterprise Resource Planning (ERP) systems; 17% use a module added on to the ERP system or a third party offering, with 3% outsourcing the process. The remainder is a mixture of stand-alone workstations, software designed for their specific industry, and a wide variety of packaged software.

The Aberdeen Group in 2011 also conducted a survey of 20 US banks on the type of payables and disbursement offerings across the supply chain and the bank revenue generation, which produced the following results.

Product	Banks offering product	Bank revenue
ACH	100%	85%
Wire transfer	100%	70%
Account reconciliation	95%	35%
Cheque issuance	90%	30%
Electronic invoice presentation	40%	5%
Supplier management/liquidity	30%	5%

Payment services are used pretty much universally across the banks. The electronic invoice presentation and payment services and the supply chain are offered by approximately a third of banks. One reason could be that the level of bank revenue is significantly less than what can be achieved through the payment products. These two areas are complex, and absorb a large amount of manual resource and demand higher pricing that is difficult to justify.

Supplier finance

In the UK, a number of banks offer supplier finance to enable major corporate buyers to offer through their bank suppliers, most probably SMEs, cash for approved invoices. The major corporate needs a credit rating of BBB or better to be part of the program. Accountants also to confirm this program does not increase the major corporate debt on the balance sheet.

The physical supply chain

Products are being manufactured in one country and sold to another country. As a result, uniform standards and formats are evolving, as is the automation of the accompanying paperwork. The following is taking place:

- More than 50% of goods by value are delivered by air, often days before the cash is moved;
- Common standards for documentation are beginning to appear across the various standard setting groups;
- Electronic preparation of documents (the move from paper to electronic) is being strongly encouraged, which eliminates errors and omissions;
- The process is becoming increasingly transparent.

The electronic financial supply chain

As the products are being made, the money involved in the manufacturing and transportation of them follows them. Each party in the chain requires payment or guarantee of payment before moving the products. The following improvements can be seen:

- Payments delivered by banks range from same day to three days;
- The opportunity to finance collateral and invoicing cross-border;
- The ability to move the financing with the goods, i.e. from buyer to seller to buyer;
- The process is becoming increasing transparency across the whole flow, both bilateral and multilateral.

Technology creates efficiency

The complexity of the supply chain creates difficulties in achieving standard workflow control when manual activities occur or are introduced. Often the manual activities result in work-around in the financial flow. This often results in ineffective cash management positions as the process has become opaque. Cash movements then become unpredictable. Ongoing operational efficiencies are created by establishing open standards and using technology that prompts for the right data at the start of the process chain. The operational efficiencies include STP (straight through processing), which, in turn, leads to predictable cash flow.

The introduction of new Extensible Markup Language (XML) based payment initiation message, combined with the associated advices and bank statement, beings to address components of the business and bank messaging – see further below and Chapter 3) The XML approach helps eliminate the use of proprietary bank standards and provides the necessary data consistency for banks to provide debit advice and financial statements.

Figure 11.1: Supply chain growth

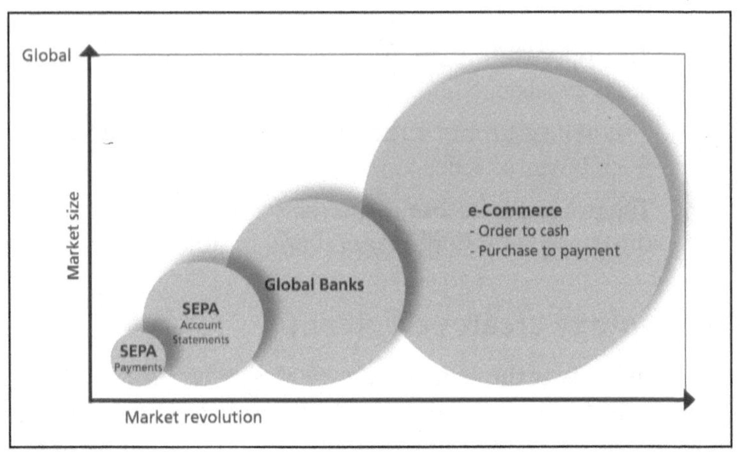

Source: XMLdation

Finally, there is a legal commitment on the banking community to support banking specific BIC (Bank Identity Codes) and IBAN (International Banking Account Numbers), which are unique strings of alphanumeric characters. Ultimately these strings need to pass through the many underlying clearing systems. The new banking codes, if correctly used, STP transactions, automation of the reconciliation process will greatly improve the timeliness of the payment.

Logistics and the supply chain

There is recognition among buyers that they cannot afford to have goods in transit or inventory for any extended length of time. In the UK, for example, the entire country's petrol supply at service stations is about seven days. The cost of inventory carry is not economically prudent, as duty has to be paid immediately (duties in the UK are over 80% of the price of the fuel). Not only does the cost of inventory accelerate the movement of goods to 'just in time' production and marketing, but the party that owns the goods and at what stage also changes. In addition, by reducing the number of stockholding centres, the savings on inventory can be substantial. In the US, for example, the inventory carrying cost as a percentage of the gross domestic product fell from some 8% in 1980 to slightly under 4% by 2000, freeing cash to invest in other ventures.

Supply chains and the role of the financial services industry

Recognising the need for an all-encompassing approach to a supply chain, many large sophisticated companies no longer accept the provision of banking services on an individual product basis. Banks that fail to provide an holistic approach to the supply chain will put at risk any existing payments, cash management, trade finance, foreign exchange and other services provided to supply chain members.

Banks are getting much closer to the supply chains of their customers and provide many non-traditional services that may include:

- A broad range of products to mitigate the risks across the supply chain;
- Investments that support the supply chains;
- Same-day cross-border payments;
- XML-based messaging to support changes in the supply chain;
- Daily reconciliation of transactions involving payments and receivables;
- Online cash forecasting;
- Electronic document preparation services.

Information obtained throughout the process is stored, reused and passed on to bring about even greater efficiencies throughout the process.

Automation and standards

The supply chain for the larger companies represents a challenge for all parties to make it as liquid as possible. To do so the supply chain has to move from physical to electronic.

Figure 11.2: Supply chain management

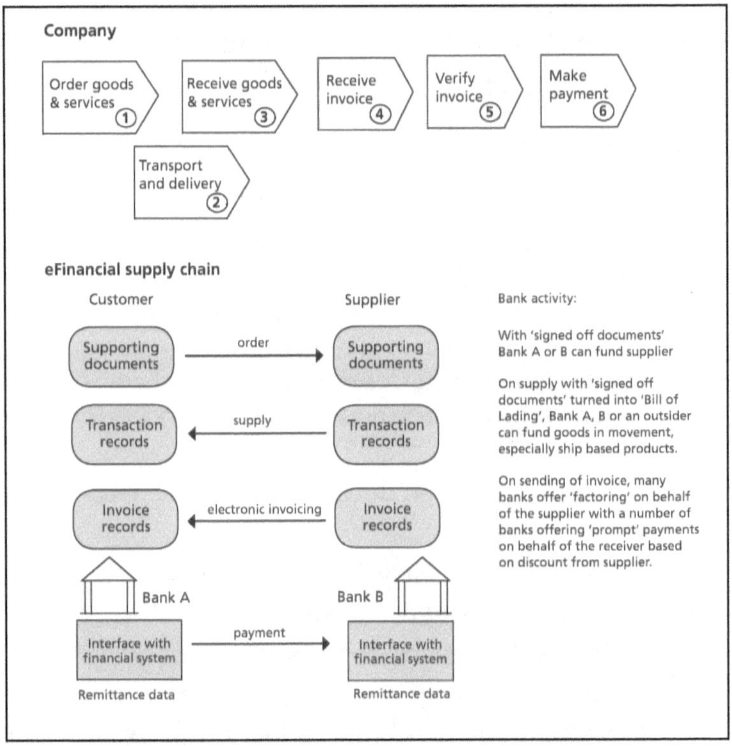

Company

Order goods & services ①
Receive goods & services ③
Receive invoice ④
Verify invoice ⑤
Make payment ⑥
Transport and delivery ②

eFinancial supply chain

Customer
Supplier

Supporting documents — order → Supporting documents
Transaction records ← supply — Transaction records
Invoice records ← electronic invoicing — Invoice records
Bank A
Bank B
Interface with financial system — payment → Interface with financial system
Remittance data
Remittance data

Bank activity:

With 'signed off documents' Bank A or B can fund supplier

On supply with 'signed off documents' turned into 'Bill of Lading', Bank A, B or an outsider can fund goods in movement, especially ship based products.

On sending of invoice, many banks offer 'factoring' on behalf of the supplier with a number of banks offering 'prompt' payments on behalf of the receiver based on discount from supplier.

Source: IBS Publishing

The introduction of the XML-based payment initiation message, combined with the associated advices and bank statements, addresses one of the three core components of the client-to-bank interface (the other two being the underlying file security and the communication interfaces). As the banking community supports this new standard, this will enable the business to use more than one bank. In simple terms, the business now has the required portability and is no longer locked into a bank through proprietary standards. However, banks' legacy internal infrastructure technologies make disconnecting from proprietary standards a slow process.

The underlying message structure has been designed to enable the business community to maximise its STP rates by clearly defining what information is required to facilitate automated processing. The XML message definition also provides the required data consistency around the debit advice and financial statements. Finally, there is a commitment from the banking community to support the provision of a unique18-character Uniform Resource Identifier (URI) in which the underlying clearing systems have the required capabilities to pass along. The changes provide the opportunity to automate the reconciliation process through the receipt of the unique reference indicator and to introduce standard, automated workflow control.

Collectively, these changes will enable the business community to achieve operational efficiencies through the elimination of the manual reconciliation process, which typically can require three to five days for the application of funds. Ultimately, in order to gain ultimate efficiencies, the reconciliation process should occur daily.

This then allows the invoices to be quickly turned into cash. Each invoice is tracked by sales days outstanding and the cost if it was an 8.5% per annum loan or through the use of invoice financing at 25.5% per annum.

Figure 11.3: Sales days outstanding

Classic dunning

Days	0-30	31-60	61-90	91-120	121-150	151-180	180+*
Month (dunning)	1	2	3	4	5	6	write-off

*Write-off policy for many companies

Cost of £100,000 in bills outstanding

Days	0-30	31-60	61-90	91-120	121-150	151-180
Cost:						
Loan	700	1,400	2,100	2,800	3,500	4,200
Invoice financing	2,100	4,200	6,300	8,400	10,500	12,600

Assuming:
1) Cost of 8.5% loan rate to the company.
Cost of money to each company is different as is cost of money by country.
2) Invoice finance of 25.5%

Note:
The company is extending credit to the supplier through sales days outstanding. A number of companies offer a discount for prompt payment, uasually within 10 days.

Source: IBS Publishing

The difference is that cost is based on the cash needs of the supplier. A cash-rich or poorly managed A/R results in an opportunity cost of £2,100 after 90 days. The company financing the invoice will charge £6,300 for the same timeframe.

The supply chain for an investment grade company can use the advantage of their credit rating to support their clients through a bank willing to work with them.

Figure 11.4: Supply chain financing for large companies

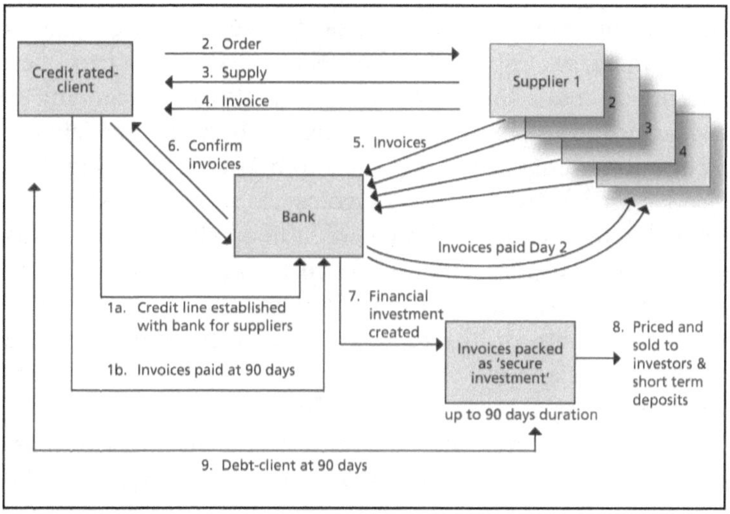

Source: Author

Figure 11.5: Accounts receivable financing

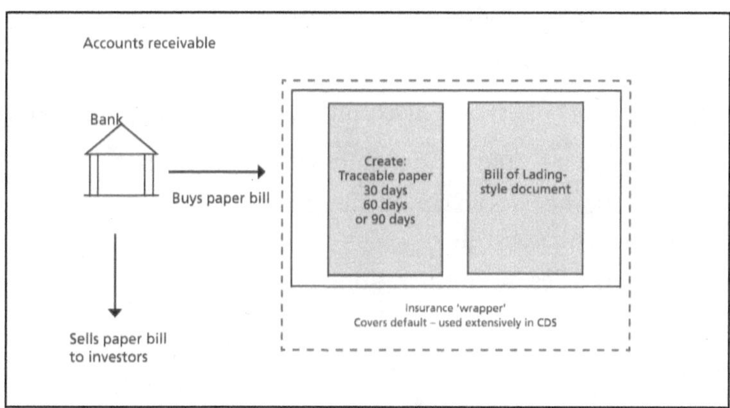

Source: IBS Publishing

Invoice financing

In times of tight credit, the use of invoice financing in all its forms increases, especially when banks do not want to open additional credit lines on their books. Invoice financing is riskier; for example, fraud in terms of 'fresh air' invoicing is a common event used by suppliers to boost the cash flow. It is also labour-intensive, as each invoice has to be verified, so the interest rates are higher than a credit line, reflecting the additional administration and the risk costs in the process.

Corporations with good credit ratings tend to pay all in 2–3% per month on the money extended. In addition to the credit reports and the credit assessment, Personal Guarantees (PGs) are often also required (see Chapter 7).

Invoice financing comes in a variety of forms; the two most common are invoice factoring and invoice discounting. The difference is that in invoice discounting, the financial company is kept confidential and the suppler (biller) performs the back-office functions of:

- Chasing the invoice for payment;
- Providing monthly statements;
- Cash allocation.

The benefits of invoice discounting for the three parties are:

- Supplier – sole relationship with the customer;
- Customer – no changes internal procedures; no changes in credit control;
- Bank – less administration.

Figure 11.6: Invoice factoring

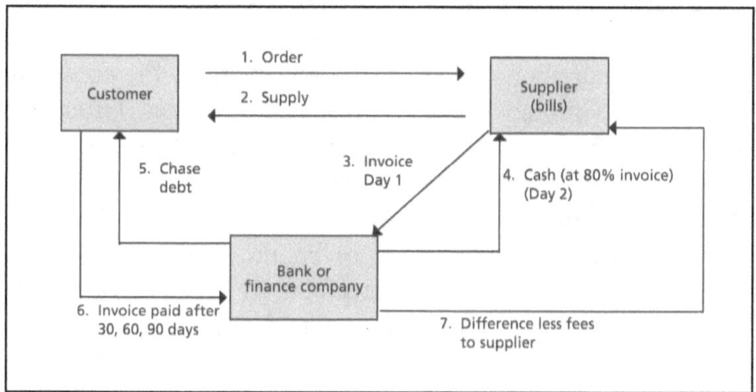

Source: Author

Figure 11.7: Invoice discounting

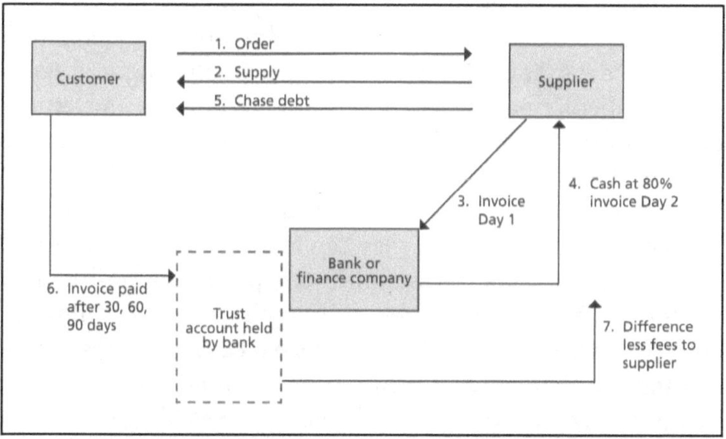

Source: Author

A bank (or finance company) takes a view on the invoices being generated by the supplier. These are checked for validity and often an additional check is made to determine who the customer is and their credit rating. The amounts requested are compared against the supplier's credit rating and within the conditions agreed to at account set-up. The bank issues a credit to a level somewhat below the value of the invoice. For example, a £10,000 invoice often is reduced by 20% and the £8,000 paid to the supplier. The money is advanced to the company and offset as money comes in from the invoices. Often the money coming into the bank is kept in a separate account, reconciled with the invoices outstanding, and then passed onto the client's account.

Value dating on the money being received in the bank's account for invoice factored invoicing is first posted to the company's 'in trust' bank account and then money moved once the payment clearing period is over. Then and only then is the money 'factored' reduced.

Factoring charges include a percentage of the invoice and/or interest charged on monies outstanding. The reason it works is that the bank provides the money to the company upfront while the suppler waits for the invoice to be paid. Payment is most often contractually set at 30 days, but often this is extended to 60 or 90 days. Some industries, such as publishing, can go to 120 days before payments are received. Wholesale movement of terms for a company from, e.g. 90 to 120 days, reflects the deteriorating financial health of the company. Suppliers experiencing such a situation need to decide whether to continue to supply and whether or not they can recover the 30 days of free credit in the future. The supplier company relationship also plays its part. In difficult times the suppliers tend to simply go along and make the appropriate internal cash decisions. Often a company experiencing some degree of financial difficulties will part-pay an invoice. This is referred to as 'throwing them a bone'.

Historically, the way banks and businesses measure the performance of accounts receivables is in days out standing (DOS) or sales days outstanding (SDO). It is not unusually for certain industries, e.g. retailing, to have a norm of 90 days from point of payment to receipt of money. This way the suppliers indirectly provide the cash for the retailer to manage the business. The product is sold from Day 1 for cash or on a credit card and then paid in total on Day 90. This is termed 'negative working capital' and used by businesses that generate cash straight away, for example, retail chains such as Zara.

The EU and other governments are trying to establish standards for the timeframe between invoice and payment. The goal is to have a 30-day standard. The UK government has key performance indicators (KPIs) for many of its services; the NHS (National Health Service) KPI is to pay invoices in 30 days. The current level is around 80% are paid in that timeframe. The issue at hand is that one person orders the product, it is delivered to one location, and a third person pays the invoice. The time taken to verify delivery and complete the administration for payment to be made can take over 30 days.

Many companies offer a discount on their charges if the payment is received within an agreed timeframe. This can be a discount from 2–5% if payment is received in 10 days.

E-invoicing

Electronic invoicing (e-invoicing) is the electronic transfer of invoice information (data on billing and payment) between business partners (supplier and buyer). It is part of the supply chain linking the company's internal processes with the payment systems. The EU estimates that replacing paper invoices with electronic generated invoices can save €64.5 billion per year for businesses. The issue has been the legal and infrastructure challenges by country and within the corporate internal environments. The EU has a goal to make e-invoicing the norm rather than the largely manual process it is today through the use of standards including ISO 20022.

E-invoicing provides massive cost savings for large company supply chain management, where costs can be as much as €60 per received invoice. Any e-invoice solution can be of immediate added value to customers in terms of faster payment, especially if it requires no major investment in their infrastructure.

E-invoicing is suitable for companies of all sizes, and implementing it in the internal system can be simple and economical. It also brings the following advantages:

- E-invoice processing significantly reduces invoicing costs;
- The number of invoicing errors is reduced because the invoice information is delivered to the customer after being fully checked automatically;
- Delivery of e-invoices to customers is fast;
- E-invoicing cuts down the use of paper and fuel as printing and transportation are eliminated;
- The invoice can be processed automatically with little or no rekeying of data.

Figure 11.8: Paper vs e-invoicing

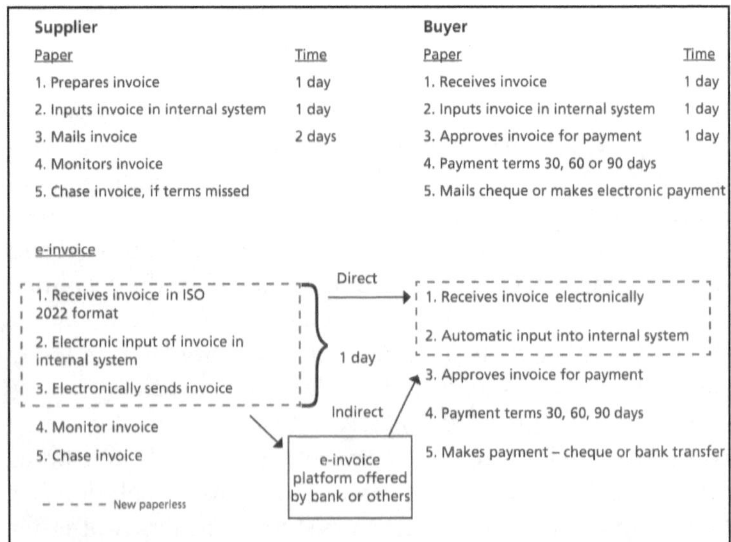

Source: Author

Global adoption of e-invoicing

While e-invoicing adoption is growing at 35% annually in Europe, it has a long way to go in terms of dominant market share. Scandinavia leads Europe, with 15% of all invoices being issued electronically.

In addition, European e-invoicing service providers recently created a trade association to represent the industry in the public policy debate, and to jointly carry out projects in the cooperative space and promote adoption. In other global regions, progress is being achieved. Key examples are Brazil and Mexico, where the government sector is leading the way, as well as North America and the Asia-Pacific regions.

The Finnish state agencies currently handle 13 million sales invoices and 1.9 million purchase invoices annually, and have over 230,000 suppliers on their database. The Finnish Treasury estimates that incoming paper invoices costs €30-50 for the receiving company. Companies can reduce these costs to €10 by semi-automating the invoice process, and reduce further down to just €1 by fully automating the process – a significant level of savings when applied across all invoices the government sends and receives. A recent report from the Federation of Finnish Financial Services estimates that, by switching from paper to electronic invoices, there is a 43% time saving per outgoing invoice and 50% for an incoming invoice. In addition, the report found that the carbon footprint for an outgoing e-invoice is less than half of that of an outgoing paper invoice.

In Europe, there are similar initiatives ongoing in Sweden and Denmark. In Mexico it is now mandatory to issue invoices electronically if the invoice sum is higher than 2,000 pesos, and, since 1 January 2011, businesses are required to perform regulatory compliance checks for senders' and receivers' invoices.

Changing supplier and buyer processes

The major block for e-invoicing is the changes needed to supplier and buyer processes. E-invoicing has been around for many years, with the two biggest and earliest proponents being General Electric (GE) and General Motors. These companies created the EDIFACT standard, but apart from a few major companies there was little uptake. Suppliers doing business with these two companies had to send in their invoices in prescribed formats as part of the terms and conditions of the contract. Basically, if there was no electronic format, then no payment of the invoice was made. The suppliers therefore had to adopt their internal systems to be EDIFACT compliant.

Bill payment in the US

Bill paying in the US has set of procedures established by the National Automated Clearing Houses Association (NACHA). The standard formats and intra-operability rules allow banks to offer a multibank option for businesses. The ACH payment message formats allow banks, billers and e-billing provider to standardise transactions. Business can now present bills in standard format through multiple banks so their customers can view and pay their bills though their own online banking site via PC or mobile phone.

The goal has always been to reduce the paperwork associated with accounts receivables and payables. The bills can be emailed to a central paying agent, for example, Citibank, by the company. The client then logs in and sees the bills to be paid. Payment can then be made electronically. Consumers in the US pay over 50% of the bills they receive electronically each month in 2011 and this trend is estimated to grow 7% in 2012. The consumers use the internet to locate their bill and then pay it online. Basically the billers post their invoices on line and e-mail or text the buyers. The buyers log on through a secure web site and pay their invoice. The buyer often has to go to many web sites to pay for many different bills.

The US company issues electronic invoices virtually 100% of the time. Of these invoices only 43% are paid in the same manner as the consumer. The reason for this is that the company has to integrate e-billing and e-payment technologies into existing processes and technologies. The adoption of e-procurement and Financial Electronic Data Interchange (FEDI) technologies is only financially viable with the larger businesses.

Citi processes nearly $5 billion per annum in bill payments through their electronic invoice presentation and payment (EIPP). The platform also allows any disputes to be settled online. Citi has noticed that on average Sales Days Outstanding can be reduced by 10 days. In addition, the dispute rate drops by 45%. The electronic cost is significantly lower than the range of $0.50 to $0.90 per transaction for the paper equivalent. Electronic payment is also faster – two days against five to seven for a cheque – and electronic payments have lower delinquency rates.

The future

The automation of the supply chain will continue. The level of capital trapped within the chain needs to be released and a community approach by industry bodies is probably needed. SWIFT, the banking infrastructure provider, has worked on a Trade Utility platform and its acceptance has been slow.

The really large companies with many suppliers can use their often-excellent credit rating to facilitate invoice financing for their suppliers from their bank. The banks encourage such initiatives as they can create the funding needed to liquefy the supply chain by selling high qualified credit rated corporate paper to other corporate treasurers with surplus cash.

By balancing the needs of businesses with surplus cash and those in need of cash in a secure and credit-sound way with a trusted third party, the money in the supply chain can be released.

SMEs tend to be at the bottom of the food chain, and working as a team through trade organisations may bring their liquidity trapped in the supply chain to the forefront. The best approach is to work with BBB or greater credit-rated companies and see if they could provide a supplier credit program. SMEs should know the level of their working capital and how long it is outstanding. They should also know if they are being paid as promptly if they are working for clients with government contracts.

CHAPTER 12
ILLIQUID MANAGEMENT

Questions for SME directors

- We are where we are now, and how do we become liquid again?
- What is the best way to keep the cash flowing, retaining the assets and handling the creditors, while undergoing a significant change in course?
- Have we been trading while insolvent?

Key considerations

- Knowing how to handle bankruptcy;
- Option of pre-pack administration.

Illiquidity is where there is a lack of cash. A company can be asset-rich yet unable to continue unless cash is found. An illiquid asset is one that cannot be easily sold or exchanged quickly for cash without a substantial drop in value. The reason is a lack of buyers or investors ready to take over these assets in total or in part. Assets which are slow to move include real estate, private investments and publicly quoted companies and bonds with no liquidity – i.e., shares and bonds that have little or no trading. The lack of trading in a particular security reflects a lack of demand. Hence when those securities are put on the market for sale the price drops until a buyer can be found.

In October 2008, Royal Bank of Scotland failed and was part nationalised. From 7 October it relied on the Bank of England for its funding. On 13 October, the UK government announced it would provide up to £20 billion of new equity to recapitalise RBS. Subsequent increases in capital brought the total to £25.5 billion, reflecting the lack of control, reporting and understanding of the fund allocation within the company.

In the UK, it is illegal to trade while insolvent. In other words, if there is no money in the accounts, then adding new debtors is against the law. For major companies reaching this point, there are avenues to keep the company alive while the credit issues are addressed. Governments will save very few companies and only those critical to that nation. The financial crisis was a new experience, resulting in countries investing taxpayers' money to prevent banks from going into liquidation and thus saving the global financial system – failure to do so could have sparked another Great Depression.

Like the UK did for RBS, governments may save an important few from bankruptcy, but for the rest with poor and deteriorating financials, receivership (someone looking after the company), restructuring (basically putting the good parts into a subsidiary and trying to offload it – the classic 'good company' and 'bad company'), or bankruptcy awaits. The value of RBS in February 2012 was quoted on the market as £16.6

billion. The UK government owns 83%, worth £13.7 billion, a substantial book loss at this time.

What the UK government did was to give time to RBS while it sorted out the banking community so that this event, if it happened again, could be handled with a lower level and immediacy of government support. That is to say, banks would be allowed to fail, as failure in the future could be measured and its impact assessed against the financial system. But time is an important consideration, and by estimating the patience of the creditors, a sense of how long it will take to correct the situation emerges. Here a potential issue is that the creditors may well force the SME to act quickly.

The timeframe available is a mixture of:

- Ongoing expenses – how much cash is really needed from the company. Can the executives and staff take a voluntary reduction during the illiquid period? People tend to be amongst the top expense items, so it is an interactive process before the situation becomes untenable. Will the existing suppliers continue with minimum payments? Often, creditors force the company to take dramatic action by demanding being paid immediately and in full.
- Lack of reserves – an unanticipated event occurs that requires cash. Here a cash cushion ranging from three months to a year is most helpful. If there are no reserves, payment has to come out of ongoing revenues, which may be the event itself – for example, a major client cancelling a significant order.
- Future committed expense – here an event where money is due by a certain time occurs. The money needed is often conditional on various terms and conditions. For example, breaking banking covenants often happens when a company is moving into an illiquid state.

- State of the assets and liabilities – having an inventory or portfolio of what assets are where and their liquidity (see the investment pyramid and the credit ladder, Chapter 7) is a great help in establishing where the liquidity is going to come from. It can also give hope to the creditors if a particular asset is being sold and money raised will be coming straight to them. Some assets are simple 'sunk costs'. The assets cost a lot of money in the first place and are recorded on the books at a figure which is now not achievable. This is true of technology hardware, for example. Computers owned for a few years are worth next to zero but vital to the business, hence a sunk cost.
- Financial engineering – reviewing the assets and liabilities to see where adjusting the cash flows can generate extra cash, for example, using asset-based financing or refinancing a loan.

When the above activities have been tried and there is no solution, then bankruptcy comes into play. For the investor or creditor, the chances of retrieving all the money are slim. Often it is pennies on the pound or cents on the dollar. In addition, there is often a hierarchy of who is to be paid first, second, third and so forth. The bank often has first call over any loans they have made, taking the number one slot in the pecking order.

Bankruptcy

Bankruptcy is one way of dealing with debts that cannot be met and the creditors are unsympathetic to the situation. Each country has its own procedures and legal requirements.

Bankruptcy is a form of insolvency and therefore debts need to outweigh assets. There are a number of approaches in this situation. Bankruptcy involves the handing over of assets to help pay off the debtors under a court partition. A trustee to administer this activity can be nominated by the court (Official

Receiver) or an insolvency practitioner (an authorised debt specialist) appointed by the directors. Once the court order has been served, the creditors have to deal with the trustee as well as the debtor. The trustee is there to ring-fence the financial situation and resolve it in the best way possible.

For businesses that enter bankruptcy, it means the end of the business and the dismissal of employees. It happens suddenly, often with little warning. The receiver calls a meeting of the staff, explains the situation and then tells everyone to go home. The Official Receiver in the UK will advertise the bankruptcy in the 'London Gazette'.

Subsidiaries in the UK

The UK permits a business to put a subsidiary into bankruptcy without affecting the company parent. This does affect how the UK banks look at lending to the subsidiary. The company parent may be fine credit score-wise, but the bank looks at the viability of the subsidiary. Banks will often require legal documentation around funding to the UK subsidiary to protect the credit being extended in case of default of the subsidiary.

In 2002, two companies - Carlton Television and Granada Television - owned ITVDigital, which signed a three-year deal with the UK Football League to broadcast games on terrestrial television. The cost of this deal - £315 million - became the principle cause of the two companies putting the company into administration. The Football League insisted on payment and announced through the BBC that two companies should honour the contract.

The administrators - Deloitte & Touche - tried to reach agreement between the parties. ITVDigital cut 25% in ongoing expenses through laying off people and renegotiating lower terms with suppliers, but the TV audiences and advertising revenue did not match the new cost base. ITVDigital said Carlton and Granada were not liable and the courts agreed that.

Bankruptcy in the US

In the US there are two major types of bankruptcy – Chapter 7 and Chapter 11.

Chapter 7 of the US Bankruptcy code states: "The company stops all operations and goes completely out of business. A trustee is appointed to liquidate (sell) the company's assets, and the money is used to pay off debt". The investor or creditor which have taken the least risk through collateralisation of their debt, specified levels of involvement, e.g. bonds are first in line on monies recovered. Shareholders are behind bondholders in any money coming from the sale of the company. Secured creditors may be the first in line based on the terms and conditions on the assets involved.

A company management going into Chapter 7 has very little control, as the trustee conducts that. Investors are usually the last to receive any money and often do not receive a penny.

Chapter 11 allows directors of the company to manage the business and control the bankruptcy procedure. The company expects to move out of bankruptcy and return to business as normal. Here time is given to bring about a change in fortunes and allows the debtor to restructure the pressing obligations. A work-out committee of investors and creditors is appointed to help the company reshape itself into a profitable entity. The success rate of Chapter 11 reorganisations is estimated at 10%.

A company in Chapter 11 is usually still trading often at much lower price levels on its shares and bonds than before the bankruptcy procedures. The Security and Exchange Commission (SEC) notes that bondholders stop receiving interest and principle payments and shareholders stop receiving dividends. A reshaping of the company may involve bond and share swaps. The terms on these swaps are usually non-negotiable and much lower than the initial monies involved.

Liquidation in the UK

The winding-up process

In the UK, more creditors are using winding-up orders to encourage and force payments. Any creditor with at least £750 owed to them can issue a winding-up petition. The procedure is as follows:

- File an application to the Law Court;
- The Court will determine if it is reasonable, and if so will issue a winding-up petition to the company;
- The company has seven days to resolve the petition by -
    - Paying the debt and costs in full;
    - Reaching an agreement to settle the debt;
    - Request the court to stop as, a) the debt is in dispute, or b) the filing is inaccurate;
- If the company does not respond then the winding-up petition will be advertised in the 'London Gazette'.

This is the point that winding-up of the company has started under the Insolvency Act 1986, section 129 (2). The company can still either pay the debt owed or argue that the petition is unreasonable at this stage. If the Court upholds the debt then the petition and issuance of a winding-up order is granted.

The process to close or liquidate the business then begins. A liquidator is appointed who will be responsible for closing the business. Any employees can be made redundant immediately. The liquidator will then try to sell any of the company's assets to generate cash. This cash is used to repay outstanding debts to the company creditors once the liquidator's fees have been paid.

Liquidation

Liquidation or winding-up is basically the end of the limited company as the assets are taken and sold and the company ceases to function. It is legally dead. There are three liquidation approaches:

1. Shareholder-led where there is enough assets to cover the debts;
    a. When there are not enough assets to cover the debts, the company can apply to Companies House to be closed down. Companies House publishes that announcement and creditors have three months to make a claim and stop the closure. This move then triggers a creditor-led liquidation;
2. Creditor-led when the shareholders acknowledge debt is greater than the assets.

    Either of these options can be a voluntary liquidation. A voluntary liquidation, which can be either a members' voluntary liquidation or a creditors' voluntary liquidation, is brought about by resolution of the company and is conducted by a qualified practitioner;
3. Compulsory liquidation,when the court makes an order for the company to be wound up on behalf a creditor or the directors of the company.

    In the UK the costs of putting a company into liquidation in 2012 are:

    - £1,165 deposit to the Court;
    - £220 court fee;
    - Cost of an advert in the 'London Gazette';
    - Any legal or accounting costs of professional services being used in the liquidation by the person pursuing the winding-up of the company.

The compulsory order results in the appointment of an official receiver. The receiver has the right to investigate the financial situation and the directors' behaviour to establish the cause of failure, as well as sell off the assets. The usual practice is to call a meeting of the creditors to appoint an insolvency practitioner (liquidator) when the company is of sufficient size. The official receiver then concentrates on the company and a report is made to the Secretary of State for Business, Innovation and Skills under the Company Directors Disqualification Act 1986. The report covers the conduct of the directors and recommended course of action.

An example of liquidation is the Glasgow Rangers Football Club. Under a former owner, Sir David Murphy, the 140-year-old club was sold to Craig Whyte for £1 plus liabilities. Whyte then raised up to £24 million by selling blocks of future tickets, thereby establishing a body of creditors. These creditors would later be asked to agree to a Company Voluntary Agreement to receive a percentage of the money they have advanced to the club.

The money from the future sales of the tickets was then used to pay off the most pressing debt, £18 million that was owned by Lloyds Bank. The club subsequently went into administration over an unpaid tax bill of £9 million within nine months of Whyte's ownership.

In 2000 the UK Insolvency Service banned Whyte from being a director of a British company for seven years. The assets of the club allegedly belong to Whyte's company, and may be worth millions in terms of residential and commercial property – not bad for a £1.

The previous owner, Sir David Murphy, did not fully utilise the assets at his disposal (see Chapter 5), and if he did follow Know Your Customer procedures, he chose to ignore indicators on the potential character of Whyte (see Chapter 2).

Pre-pack administration

One approach to bankruptcy is the 'pre-pack'. This covers the process of selling the assets immediately after it has gone into administration. It is a process conceived and put in place by the directors that allow the best assets of the company to pass through the administration while leaving the creditors out. It also is contingent on the directors finding the necessary funds to pay the administrator and fund the company going forward. An example of a pre-pack is Cobra Beer, which was sold to Coors immediately after Cobra Beer entered administration. While saving employee jobs as well as the brand, this move left suppliers (debtors) out of pocket by £75 million.

The future

The level of cash management needs to improve to help slow down the level of bankruptcies, as it is clear in the UK and the US there is very little money left for investors and creditors once the administrators have been paid. Most bankruptcies occur when a creditor insists on getting paid immediately and in full. Often the creditor is culpable in allowing the amount outstanding to grow too big for the company's financial well-being. With today's technology, levels of credit can be set, monitored and managed.

SMEs in illiquid situations need to restructure so incoming revenue can meet outgoing expenses. The past becomes a negotiation between the SMEs and the creditors, which may well stop the future and all loss. The SME can close the company and start again. The credit record will take a negative dive, but the courts offer protection from creditors, so intimidated by collection agencies and bailiffs is controllable.

www.ingramcontent.com/pod-product-compliance
Lightning Source LLC
LaVergne TN
LVHW091054080826
845145LV00002B/742